Kyra

Kyra

A LIFE OF
SIMPLE SURRENDER

CYNTHIA G. SMITH

REDEMPTION
PRESS

*Dedicated to Nolyn,
Ellie, and Livia.*

The Kyra Karr Foundation exists
to glorify God by serving
and supporting the local church.
All proceeds from the book and
donations to the foundation
will go to this cause.

We hope that you will
prayerfully support the
KKF's mission, and we thank you
in advance for your gifts.
To God be the glory through
the equipping of His church.

KyraKarrfoundation.com

THE KYRA KARR
———— F O U N D A T I O N ————

Contents

Foreword

*T*here are times in our lives when we meet a person who impacts us in a significant way and whose influence has an eternal impact on our lives. Kyra Carp Karr had such an impact on me.

To know Kyra was to love and learn from Kyra. I did both.

Maybe you're thinking, that you didn't know her. Why should you keep reading this book? Then let me suggest that you need to read it for inspiration. She will become like a dear friend to you as you read of her family, her faith, her journey, her fears, and the impact she made on everyone around her.

She will encourage you to face what overwhelms you and to seek the One who knows everything about you and created you with purpose to do amazing things.

Maybe, like Kyra, you are a daughter, sister, wife, or mother. Kyra was all these things.

But her story is not just for women. It's for all of us who

are seeking to know more about a God we cannot see. It is for those who are willing to explore the possibility of enjoying a relationship with Him that might make an impact on this world. This book is for you.

Kyra's honest journal entries will reveal the spiritual, emotional, and relational struggles in various seasons of her life and demonstrate how God was the source of her strength and joy in every situation.

I encourage you to turn the pages and be inspired by Kyra's both ordinary and extraordinary life.

We were all built by design for a divine purpose. Maybe you've lost sight of that and could use a reminder. Or maybe you don't agree but are willing to take a journey to explore the possibility.

Either way, you will not be disappointed. May your Creator meet you on the pages of this book and blow a fresh wind over your life.

Thank you, Kyra, for leaving us all your legacy of faith, hope, and love.

Kim Lewis
Executive Director of Bartow Family Resources
Cartersville, Georgia

1

The Early Morning Call

❦

The phone had been on my bedside table all night on silent. At seven in the morning, I picked it up and saw that I had some missed calls. The first one was from my close friend Kim Lewis. Kim and I have a thirty-year-old friendship, and we also enjoyed working together at Bartow Family Resources in Cartersville, Georgia.

I called Kim back right away. I will never forget the pause before she said, "Cindy, Kyra has been killed in a car accident. It happened late last night." My mind rebelled against the words I was hearing. Kim and I wept together for a few minutes before hanging up. This could not be happening!

As I ended the call with my friend, I focused on the memory of just a few days before when Kim gave Kyra Karr a tour of Bartow Family Resources. Kim had brought Kyra to my office. All three of us high fived over the dream of setting up a type of Bartow Family Resources Center in Rome, Italy, where Kyra and her husband served as missionaries. I could still see Kyra's enthusiasm about serving in Italy. The three of us encouraged each other as we intentionally talked about valuing life here in America, Italy, and beyond.

The second thought was for Kyra's husband, Reid, and their three daughters, Nolyn, Ellie, and Livia. Then I thought of Kyra's parents, Karen and Joe, and her sisters, Chelsey and Sydney. *How were they doing?* I thought about my friend Alexis, Reid's sister, and his mom, Janet. What could I do, I wondered? How could I let my friend Karen know of my sorrow for her great loss?

The day was full of phone calls to inform our church members of the tragedy. The ones who did not personally know Kyra responded, "Is that the missionary who the church prayed for on Sunday night?" Each time, I replied, "Yes, it was Kyra."

A huge knot grabbed my stomach as I remembered when Kyra, Reid, and their daughters had been prayed for during the church service just a few nights ago. The pastors prayed for Kyra and Reid to be protected as they flew back to Italy and that God would bless their work in serving the Italian people. My thoughts began racing. *Well, a lot of good that prayer did! Kyra was not protected in this accident, and she will not be going back to Italy!*

That evening a prayer meeting was held at Dellinger Park in Cartersville. Friends prayed for Reid, the girls, Karen, Joe, the whole family, and the Italian people, who would deeply miss Kyra. The thirty people who held hands in the middle of the football and track field embodied the church and community. They gathered to share the Carp and Karr families' grief.

During the prayer meeting, I shared about my visit to Rome just two years before, where I saw Kyra in action serving her family and Italian neighbors. I told of my awe of Kyra as I walked beside her on our daily walks to the Italian supermarket. She carried Livia in a front carry pouch as she pushed Ellie in a stroller and as Nolyn walked beside us. I had tried not to be too wide-eyed as I watched Kyra speak Italian to her neighbors and those she passed in the street. Her blonde hair stood out there, but more than that her smile made people do a double take.

The next few days after Kyra's death were taxing for the family as, between the visitation and the funeral service, about a thousand people spent time with them. After the service, a friend, Lisa Seabolt Bagnell, said that she had only been to one other funeral that was as glorifying to God as Kyra's, and that was the funeral of Philip Karr, Reid's dad, twenty years earlier.

Kyra's funeral—I like to call it a celebration of her life—was an experience that I will always remember. Perhaps not all the details from that day were imprinted in my memory, but I was deeply affected when Reid stood to thank everyone for all the outpouring of love and then thanked God for Kyra's life. Kyra's daddy, Joe, stood up and spoke about how hard this loss was but that God was good. I was amazed that he could say, "God is good." Kyra's sister said the same thing: "God is good."

Then Kyra's friend Katie said, "Kyra was not of this world. She was made for heaven."

Laura, another friend, also expressed her own trust in God in the midst of great loss.

I struggled to resolve the anger I felt. My head knowledge knew God was good, but how could this tragedy be good? I must be honest; I could not see God's goodness in it. I wanted answers. *Why Kyra?* Then other questions crossed my mind. *Will Reid take the girls back to Italy without Kyra?* I wondered, *What is it about Reid, this family, and Kyra's friends that gives them strength to stand in front of hundreds of people and proclaim their love and trust in a sovereign God?*

That last question put me on a journey. I wanted to understand Kyra more deeply and come to a place of peace about her death. I wanted to comfort Kyra's family with a book and dedicate it to Kyra's three daughters. I wanted people in Italy to know about the American woman who loved them so much that she left her home country to make theirs her own. I was intrigued to understand how her family trusted Jesus in their darkest moments.

The writing of this book involved a six-year personal journey to gain understanding and insight into this exceptional young woman and her family. I spoke with Kyra's family, interviewed her friends, and read her journals. I traveled to Italy to visit her family, friends, and church family there.

I invite you to read about her life through this assortment of stories, devotions based on lessons from her life, and excerpts from her journal. I've also included some of the recipes that she enjoyed cooking, as she practiced her gift of hospitality. If she were here, she would not only cook for you and tell you her stories, but she would also tell you the story of her Savior. Her walk with God was not a religion full of rules . . . it was a relationship full of grace and mercy. A relationship that called her to walk away from her pride and to confidently sprint toward a life of surrender.

2

Foundational Love

Kyra's Foundation

Everyone loves a love story—a story of two people who meet, fall in love, commit their lives to one another, and somehow figure out how to sustain that love as they navigate the challenges of life. Yet the success of a marriage is built on far more than any fairy-tale romance portrayed by Hollywood and popular books or magazines.

I believe that, at its core, a successful marriage has its roots in the respective families that nurtured each partner and demonstrated how to love and whom to love. For Reid and Kyra, the baseline for their relationship was the love of Jesus, which had been cultivated by parents who lived out the truth of Jesus Christ's sacrificial love before their children.

Kyra loved her husband, but he was not her first love. At Kyra's celebration of life on August 19, 2015, Reid offered this testimony:

The single most important thing in Kyra's life was her relationship with Jesus Christ. That is who she was. It made her who she was. It made her the friend that she was to so many of you, the sister to her sisters, the daughter to Joe and Karen, and the incredible mom she was to our three little girls, and the wife that she was to me.

The standard for Kyra and Reid's relationship was the love of Jesus. They related to each other through the lens of God's supernatural love based on 1 Corinthians 13.

The love that Kyra and Reid shared is best appreciated in context of their family histories, especially the stories of how their parents came to be. For Kyra's parents, Joe and Karen Carp, their romance began at an athletic shoe and apparel store convention in New Orleans. The turmoil and changes of the sixties provided the backdrop for the love story of Reid's mom and dad, Philip and Janet Karr. Each couple lived their own love story and built a legacy for Kyra and Reid.

Stepping into Sync

Times were exciting in the early eighties. Ronald Reagan was the fortieth president of the United States. Michael Jackson's music video "Thriller" was broadcast for the first time. Apple placed the Macintosh personal computer on sale in America. The TED conferences were founded. Chrysler produced the first minivans—the Dodge Caravan and the Plymouth Voyager. McDonalds introduced McNuggets, and the movies *Ghostbusters* and *The Terminator* were making big bucks at the box office. During this time in history, Joe Carp and Karen Howard met.

Their story begins at a famous New Orleans address, 601 Loyola Avenue. Anyone who lived in New Orleans knew that location as the Hyatt Regency New Orleans. The large hotel with thirty-two floors and over 1,100 guest rooms served as a popular venue for sizeable conferences. The nearby Superdome was a part of the Hyatt's complex of connected buildings. In this setting, one couple found each other.

In the winter of 1984, Foot Locker, an athletic footwear and apparel retailer, had chosen New Orleans as the location for their nationwide managers conference. At the time, the decade-old franchise was trying something a little different. Instead of only inviting male managers, women were invited to attend as well. The company was branching out to pilot Lady Foot Locker stores and planned to have these new stores managed by women. The approximately 1,200 male managers attending the conference were now going to be joined by ten or so female managers. Excitement was in the air!

Karen Howard had moved from Knoxville, Tennessee, to become a manager trainee at one of the Foot Locker stores in Chicago, Illinois. She traveled through the Chicago O'Hare Airport filled with enthusiasm and anticipation to leave the frigid temperatures of Chicago for the sunny winter weather of New Orleans. Even then, O'Hare was one of the busiest airports in the world, with thousands of passengers passing through each day. But Karen still managed to notice a certain tall blond young man in navy blue Adidas sweatpants. He walked with the air of having life all together, his stride steady and fixed. Even from a few hundred feet away, Karen spotted the stripes in his peach golf shirt.

Joe Carp also lived in Chicago and managed one of the three Foot Locker stores. The managers conferences were not new to Joe, so being a routine kind of guy, he simply stayed focused on what was ahead. Flying out of O'Hare was just a part of the plan to get from point A to point B: New Orleans and its warm, sunny atmosphere.

There was an extravagant banquet on the last night of the

Foot Locker conference. Joe remembered the previous banquets as being enjoyable. One had even featured a famous Olympian, Bruce Jenner, as a guest speaker. The room full of people at round tables set the tone for a charming and delightful evening. Joe and his fellow managers happened to be sitting at the table next to the famed Lady Foot Locker ladies. While all the women were busy in their interactions with each other, it did not take long for Joe to notice one in particular. He saw a beauty in the pretty manager-in-training that flowed from the inside out. Squinting to see her name tag, he read *Karen Howard*. Being the planner and person who knew how to strategize, Joe began to sketch out a mental formula on how to meet this young woman. Joe's mom, Lois, who'd had seven children—with Joe in the middle—had always taught her kids to enjoy their youth and not date too early. With this teaching on his mind, he had never seriously dated anyone. Somehow, Joe sensed that this was all about to change.

Nicely clad in an elegant black dress, it did not take Karen long to notice Mr. Striped Peach Golf Shirt at the next table. Yes, he was dressed differently, but even with his white shirt and tie, he was clearly the guy who had caught her attention at the airport! His name tag read *Joe Carp*.

The evening was topped off with an invitation to tour the famous Bourbon Street. In the crowd Joe had lost sight of Karen only to turn around in one of the courtyards and find her right behind him. The two began talking. Both loved talking about family and sports, and instantly a connection formed. Joe and Karen walked away from the group. They talked on the steps of the Hyatt into the night and the early hours of the next morning and soon began a relationship.

After they'd been dating a while in Chicago, Karen's new management job with Lady Foot Locker transferred her to Virginia Beach. A born and bred northerner, Joe had decided he really liked the South and its traditions. Plus, he really liked Karen. That made it easy for Joe to resign from Chicago's Foot Locker and move.

Those first four hours of talking on the steps of the Hyatt eventually led to a marriage covenant ceremony at Thalia Lynn Baptist Church in Virginia Beach, Virginia. Joe and Karen made their lifetime commitment in front of a few friends and family members. The dinner afterward reflected the fun life that the happy couple would share. The menu included boiled shrimp, which was a new kind of dish for Joe. It was not long before Joe felt crackling and sharp bits as he chewed the shrimp. It just did not seem right. Karen gently (most likely with a sweet smile) taught her new husband that the shell cover needed to come off before eating the little crustacean!

Foot Locker focused on hiring people who valued trust, quality, commitment, and respect. All these qualities helped Joe and Karen build a strong family for Kyra and her sisters, leaving them a legacy built on God's love.

Today

Joe and Karen continue to invest in their relationship with each other and in the lives of their family. They are intentional in sharing the love of Christ in their community.

Joe plays basketball with young men at parks in his community. His goal is to build relationships through playing basketball. Scores of young men and their families have been impacted by Mr. Joe's love for Jesus.

Karen opens her doors each week to host a Bible study in her home. Every Tuesday evening, women of all ages and denominations come to focus on their spiritual growth. In addition to the Bible study, the Tuesday night desserts are said to be delicious!

Selling sportswear and shoes brought Karen and Joe

together. Walking in sync has kept them together for almost four decades.

Keep Your Eyes on Jesus

Reid's parents' love story began in the mid-sixties. America was still recovering from a presidential assassination, as well as trying to grasp the magnitude and importance of the civil rights marches in Alabama. The US was involved in an unpopular war in Vietnam. The music world was turned upside down with the Beatles' debut, "I Want to Hold Your Hand." Ford produced the first Mustang, and the game show *Jeopardy* made its debut on NBC.

Yes, there was a lot going on in the United States and around the world in the sixties. However, this story focuses on an account that took place in Atlanta, Georgia, at East Point Methodist Church. Janet Haley was in seventh grade when she noticed a seventeen-year-old young man playing Joseph of Arimathea in the passion play. Her crush began on that day. Unfortunately, Janet was joined by her many friends who also had crushes on the same young actor. Philip Karr was a youth leader. He became like a big brother to all the seventh-grade girls, but unlike the other girls, Janet never got over her crush.

The age difference split the lives of Janet and Philip for about five more years. Philip attended Georgia Tech to earn one of his three engineering degrees and later joined the Marine Reserves. He also traveled through Georgia as a circuit preacher. During this season, Janet was enjoying life as a young teen.

One Sunday, Janet was singing in the choir and her date was sitting down front in the congregation. Before the service began, Janet saw Philip Karr and his date walk into the church. To Janet, it was as if the pair was walking in slow motion down the aisle. The sight of Philip with another girl triggered a physical reaction as her stomach turned flips. *What was happening?*

Soon after this, Janet's mom asked her husband if he had noticed the way Philip Karr was eyeing their daughter. The other former seventh-grade girls had also noticed how Philip looked at Janet. This caused a little tension for Janet, but it did not stop her from going out with Philip Karr. Yes, he had asked the high-school senior out. Janet had been chosen by "Joseph of Arimathea."

Philip and Janet enjoyed a fun dating life that built a strong foundation for their relationship. One date night took them to Dairy Queen. Their favorite song, "The Twelfth of Never" by Johnny Mathis, played on the car radio during the drive over. Philip ran inside the DQ to get two chocolate-covered ice cream cones. Bringing the cones back to the car, he looked in the car window and asked Janet, "When are we going to get married?"

With her beautiful brown eyes opened wide, Janet answered, "I don't know."

Even though this was not the romantic proposal that Janet had probably dreamed of, it was the way Philip Karr rolled. After Philip asked Janet's dad for permission to marry his daughter, the two set a wedding date. The Haleys were more than grateful to have Philip join the family. Janet was the oldest of four children and the only daughter. Adding one more son, especially one of Philip's caliber, brought a lot of joy to the Haley family.

The wedding ceremony took place at the same church where they had met—East Lake Methodist Church in Atlanta. It was an extremely sweltering day on July 9, 1965. Much to Mrs. Haley's chagrin, she had to water down the punch because the guests were so hot and thirsty.

After living in Pascagoula, Mississippi, for a short while, Janet and Philip moved to Chicago to train for a job through Chicago Bridge and Iron. This training would take them to Arenzano, Italy. Philip worked in Italy for eighteen months before the Georgia couple returned to Atlanta where their first daughter, Alexis, was born. The family of three moved to Clemson, North Carolina, where Philip earned his doctorate in environmental systems engineering. Robin was born five years after Alexis, and Philip Reid IV, Kyra's future husband, was born in 1979. Stacey was born just fifteen months behind Reid. In 1987 the family would grow again—this time through marriage, when eighteen-year-old Alexis married twenty-three-year-old Kyle Vance. The newlyweds were the same ages that Janet and Philip had been when they married. Everyone thought that the Philip Karr family was complete. Then the Karrs gave birth to twins in 1989. Reid was ten when Jared and Jordan were born. It was a busy life!

Celebrations and New Year's resolutions captured everyone's thoughts as 1995 made its grand entrance. Philip had just self-diagnosed himself with having Parkinson's disease after experiencing some troubling physical symptoms. Janet battled the painful emotions over the thought of her husband having Parkinson's, but Philip could still live and operate with the condition. As the youngest Cobb County city water manager that had ever been hired, Philip was at the height of his career and a sought-after speaker at Georgia Institute of Technology.

It was in this busy season that Philip began to feel the toll of health issues. Reluctantly, he took time out to go to the doctor and have some medical tests run. Just a few days later, Kyle drove Philip back home from a Georgia Tech lecture. For the first time ever, Philip had asked for a ride because he was not feeling well. Philip answered his phone during the ride home. His secretary told him that the result of his MRI was in, and his doctor wanted to see him immediately. Kyle drove Philip straight to the medical center. Slowly the doctor shared, "You have a brain tumor on the top of your brain."

In a matter-of-fact voice, Philip replied, "That's life." Somehow, he always took things in stride and knew how to face things with an unwavering faith.

Philip broke the news to Janet. "I have something to tell you." He was holding his Bible as he explained, "I have a brain tumor."

Just four months into the new year, the motion of the world stopped as Janet took in those five words. The legacy left for Reid and his family would take an even more unexpected turn.

The biopsy showed the tumor had wrapped itself all over Philip's brain. As Janet and her friends from her Bible study group waited in the hospital room, the doctor explained that the tumor was very aggressive and inoperable. Janet's first words were, "What will I ever do without him?"

For ninety days Kyle drove Philip to get radiation during his lunch break from his job at Tip Top Poultry. Philip could not walk by this time and was losing all muscle strength and control. On the twin's sixth birthday, the family helped Jared and Jordan open presents in front of their daddy. Though he could not speak or hold his head upright, he managed to wave at his youngest children.

On December 30, 1995, it was Kyle's turn to check on Philip at 3:00 a.m. Kyle woke up but did not feel a peace about going down at that time, so he waited another hour. At 4:00 a.m. he walked toward the sunroom where Philip slept. He could hear the CD that continually played in Philip's room. The words "no more sorrows, no more pain" were astound-ingly clear as Kyle entered the room to find his beloved father-in-law no longer breathing. Reid, who was sixteen years old at the time, had asked Kyle to please come get him before going to get his mom if his dad passed during the night. So Kyle awakened Reid first as promised, then Janet.

Their neighbor, Sharon Seabolt, could see the Karr home from her kitchen window. On the night that Philip passed, Sharon had been unable to sleep. She looked out the window just in time to view a bright light that filled Philip's room. The bright light caught her attention since Philip's room was normally dim. After talking to Sharon, Kyle understood why he did not have peace about going to check on Philip at 3:00—that was the time when Philip was being ushered into heaven.

Janet and their six children had remained vigilant as Philip's condition deteriorated over an eight-month period. His struggle was over. He had exchanged his battered earthly suit for a new heavenly garment.

Reid, at just sixteen years of age, had to make a choice. Would the suffering and death of his dad prevent his spiritual growth, or would it propel him forward? Would the absence of his father's everyday presence silence the biblical teachings his dad had poured into him, or would the truth become more alive?

Before Philip died, he had prayed for each of his children to find their soul mate. He saw that prayer answered for Alexis. Even though Kyra was only ten at the time of his passing, she was the beautiful answer to prayer for his son Reid.

Today

Janet continues to serve the Lord, her family, and the community. All six children are following the examples of their parents. Philip and Janet's love story built a strong legacy that is summed up in five words that Philip so often repeated that they are engraved on his tombstone: "Keep your eyes on Jesus."

3

How We Spend Our Dash

*T*his section was inspired by an email that Karen received from one of Kyra's favorite high-school teachers, Mr. Ken Foster.

> Karen, my thoughts about Kyra in the last week have been centered on the poem about the dash between birth and death. I have especially focused on the final few lines.
>
> > Remembering that this special dash
> > Might only last a little while
> >
> > So, when your eulogy is being read
> > With your life's actions to rehash
> > Would you be proud of the things they say
> > About how you spent your dash?
> > (Ellis, "The Dash," stanzas 8 and 9)

Kyra had an amazing dash. I accept God's will for Kyra's life, but I do not know if I will ever stop asking God WHY this beautiful child of God was taken from us so soon. During my forty years in education, I have lost other students who I loved, but none have touched my life the way that I have been touched by the loss of Kyra.

~ Ken Foster

The narrative of Kyra's "dash" begins with Karen's recollection of her first daughter's birth and ends with the moment she learned of her daughter's death. The stories that follow reveal the beginning of Kyra's faith walk, the early years in Cartersville, her teenage years, college days, her pivotal year, marriage, motherhood, and missions.

Although Kyra stood out, she was like each of us who struggle with everyday stresses. Yet even during mundane challenges, her honesty and humble heart brought peace to those around her. She was a giver in this world, and that is what makes each episode in her dash so meaningful.

In the Span of 11,216 Days

Every birth story is unique and holds its own type of wonder. Kyra's was no different. After admission to Virginia Beach General Hospital, Karen patiently—or maybe not so patiently—waited to meet her son. *A son? But Kyra was a girl.* Karen's doctors and nurses were sure that Karen was carrying a boy. In 1984, expectant mothers did not routinely have ultrasounds, but their friends often told them what they were having based on certain old wives' tales. Karen was told that since the baby's heartbeat was slow, she must be having a boy. The Carps thought that they would be meeting "Justin Michael," who would have the same initials as his daddy, Joe.

Karen had dreamed of what this little one inside her would bring to the world. Soon she would meet her first-born. After waiting for a few hours as labor progressed, Karen nervously pushed the help button beside her bed. As the nurse entered the room, she declared, "Honey, don't you worry, your baby is about to be born!"

On that Tuesday morning around 10:15 a.m., Joe was leaning beside Karen's head when they heard the first cry of their newborn. Joe could not see the baby at first and excitedly called out, "It's a boy!"

Then the doctor smiled. "Actually, this baby is a girl."

Kyra Lynn (Karen's initials) entered the world on November 27 at seven pounds, fifteen ounces, and twenty-one and a half inches long. Joe beamed with pride over his daughter. Karen cried with joy.

As a first-time mother, Karen wanted every newspaper and news station to shout out that a new life had just entered the world! Time stood still as Karen looked into her daughter's eyes. Hearing Kyra's first cry was like music to her soul.

Excuse Me, Nurse

In 1984 newborns stayed in a nursery with a big viewing window for all the admiring visitors. The curtains to the windows were only open at certain times. When friends and members visited, they crowded around the window, and coos and whispers of celebration bounced off the walls of the hospital hallways. Inside the nursery window, a row of newborns lay in clear plastic bassinets on wheels. Each baby was swaddled in a receiving blanket with a tiny little sweater cap on their head. Friends and families strained to see the names written on blue or pink cards located on the front of each cart.

Daddy Joe, who was normally patient, did not like the time restraints of only holding Kyra when the nurse brought her into Karen's post-partum hospital room. He wanted more time with his newborn. Joe marched right up to the nursery glass, knocked on the window, and told the nurse he wanted to come in and hold his daughter. To his surprise, the nurses quickly obliged. Daddy Joe looked proud as he confidently wore the required hospital gown and face mask to hold Kyra. Joe looked down at Kyra as he silently prayed to be the daddy she needed. Daddy holding daughter . . . all was well.

Karen and Joe repeated the birthing experience two more times. Each maternity ward visit rewarded them with another daughter: Chelsey and then Sydney who completed the trio of sisters. Joe was a passionate father providing for, praying for, and guiding each of his daughters. Karen was an exceptional mother, intentionally tending to the unique needs of each of her daughters. Together, Joe and Karen made a healthy parenting team.

The Knock on the Door

Fast forward thirty years.

Chelsey had flown in from Knoxville to spend the last evening with Kyra and her family before they left for their home in Italy the next day. Kyra's stateside visit, which only happened every two years, went by too fast. Joe, Karen, Chelsey, Reid, Kyra, and their daughters met Sydney and her husband Daniel at a favorite restaurant in Acworth, Georgia. After a fun-filled evening, the little group reluctantly said their goodbyes to Sydney and Daniel. Kyra and Reid's oldest daughter, Nolyn, got in the car with Chelsey, Karen, and Joe as Reid, Kyra, and their younger daughters, Ellie and Livia, drove away in their borrowed Toyota Tundra.

When Reid and Kyra did not return to the house in a timely manner, Chelsey and Joe went to look for them.

Before Joe could return, Karen heard a knock on their front door. Somehow she knew that when she opened the door, her life would never be the same. Trembling, Karen prayed, *Oh, Lord, what do I do?* Reluctantly she opened the door. Dr. Chris Sward, their family friend who owned the truck that Kyra and Reid had been driving, and a uniformed man whom Karen did not know, stood on the stoop in front of her.

The policeman asked, "Ma'am, can we come in?"

Karen could not take her eyes off Chris as she asked him, "Is it Kyra?"

Chris, with tears in his eyes, responded, "I am so sorry, Karen. She is gone."

Karen simply looked up into the heavens. With a broken heart, she prayed, *Lord, if you had to take her, please don't let it be for nothing.*

Karen and Joe had waited expectantly for the birth of their firstborn daughter. They were prepared to do whatever it took to protect and provide for their newborn. However, nothing could have prepared them for the moment when they knew they would never again hear Kyra's voice this side of heaven.

I have played Karen's words over and over in my mind. She was squeezed with agony as the news crushed her soul, and her first word was *Lord*?

The saying, "You never know what is in the toothpaste tube until you squeeze it," comes to my mind. I do not know who originated the toothpaste saying, but whoever said it revealed a profound truth. When something good or bad happens, our first response reveals the real us. Karen's plea was a cry to a personal God with whom she had a very personal relationship. She immediately ran to the One who knew everything about her, the One who would provide a haven where she would be heard.

Karen turned to God in both the happy and sad times in her life. She easily rejoiced in the good times and somehow learned how to rejoice in the painful seasons.

Kyra's journaled prayer reflects a faith just as solid:

> *I want to steward my time on earth wisely.*
> *May I be a blessing to my family. I pray that*
> *by your Spirit that I could do just that.*

Her heavenly Father heard that prayer. Kyra did live wisely and was a blessing to all who knew her.

He also heard Karen's prayer: *Lord, please don't let it be for nothing.* Kyra's 11,216 days on earth continue to make an unforgettable impact on those she knew as well as on those who will meet her through her life stories.

4

The Birth of Spiritual Trust

A Foundation of Trust

From the time of conception, Kyra was given an opportunity to hear about Jesus. I believe that infants are born recognizing familiar voices. With that in mind, tiny Kyra heard her mother's prayers even as she grew in the womb. She was also enrolled in what Baptists call the "cradle roll." That simply meant that when Karen told the church she was pregnant, the unborn baby was immediately assigned to a newborn Sunday school class. At six weeks of age, Kyra was welcomed into her church teacher's arms.

Not every child is born into a family that recognizes the importance of making spiritual health a priority. But from an early age, Kyra grasped the meaning of what it meant to be a Christ follower—one who wanted to please God with all her heart.

Kyra's First Bible

Kyra quickly grew into a little girl who loved her school and all that it included, from scholastics to social events. She also loved church. One of Joe and Karen's favorite memories from the "little girl" season is when Kyra got her first Bible at their church in Memphis, Tennessee, where the Carps lived for a few years.

Kyra was one of over a hundred wiggly, excited, wide-eyed first graders who lined the wide hallway with their Sunday school teachers. Keeping order of the eager children who were about to make their grand entrance was no easy task. The teachers watched their little charges in hopes that time would move quickly.

Finally, it was time to enter the sanctuary of Bellevue Baptist Church, where the legendary Adrian Rogers served as pastor. There was a lot of smiling and waving that morning as each child looked for their family members. These first graders were just learning to read, so it was time for each of them to receive their very own Bible.

Karen and Joe beamed with joy as they spotted Kyra Lynn bouncing in. Kyra sat on the front row. Her blonde hair and contagious smile, with front teeth missing, were winsome, even at six years old.

Dr. Adrian Rogers, who at that time had pastored Bellevue Baptist for thirty-three years, introduced himself and welcomed everyone to the service. His booming voice captivated everyone in the sanctuary as he spoke of God's love for children. He shared that Bellevue wanted to help each first grader start off their journey with a light for their life: the Word of God. He focused on Psalm 119:105: "Your word is a lamp for my feet, a light on my path." After Dr. Rogers completed his dedication speech, he presented each child, including Kyra, with their Bible.

Kyra held up her new Bible for her parents to see as they picked her up from class. Joe and Karen exclaimed over her Bible, letting her know it was the greatest Book for her to read. The Bible had been autographed by Dr. Adrian Rogers.

Even at a young age, Kyra was described as intelligent and rational. She was a natural critical thinker. She knew there was more to life than what met the human eye.

The Bible became a source of strength for Kyra as she became an adult. When Kyra had feelings of bitterness toward another person, she would write down Bible verses on forgiveness. When she became afraid, she wrote down verses that combated fear. When Kyra became a wife and then a mother, she copied verses that would give her strength for the journey.

On that day in Memphis when the first graders received their Bibles, it set a path for each child. For Kyra, the Bible became a treasure. She knew that it had a value that could not be measured in dollars. She knew that it held answers to life's deepest questions, and she read it as if it was speaking only to her.

Baptism

When Kyra was nine years old, God's love reached out to her spirit, and she responded with simple faith. She went to her parents and asked them to help her figure out what was going on inside her heart. She felt a pull toward the Jesus she had been reading about since she was six years old. Somehow she knew that she could not live the way the Bible asked her to without help from Jesus. She was deeply sorry for her behavior toward others. Even at nine, she knew she wanted to change and live a good life that honored God.

Kyra's parents wanted to make sure she was not

expressing her belief in Jesus just because she thought they expected it. It became clear to them that their daughter's faith was genuine. Kyra sincerely asked God's forgiveness for the ways she disobeyed Him. They saw that she was beginning to comprehend that Jesus came to earth to show us God, while also starting to grasp the significance of His death, burial, resurrection, and ascension. At the tender age of nine, Kyra invited Jesus to be the guide of her life.

Karen made an appointment for Kyra to talk to Bobby Atkins, the pastor of the church they were attending at the time. Pastor Bobby was convinced that Kyra was ready to make a public declaration of the decision she had made privately. Kyra was baptized at Silverdale Baptist Church in Chattanooga, Tennessee. The baptism took place at a morning service in the baptism pool located at the front of the church above the choir loft.

Pastor Bobby welcomed Kyra into the baptism pool while Karen waited for her on the other side. He asked Kyra, "Do you believe that Jesus is the Son of God? And do you trust Jesus as your Savior and commit to obey Jesus as your Lord?"

With a firm decisiveness, Kyra answered, "Yes, I do."

Right before immersing Kyra's small frame under water, Pastor Bobby said, "On the profession of your faith in Jesus Christ as your Lord and Savior, and in obedience to His command, I now baptize you in the name of the Father, and of the Son, and of the Holy Spirit." As Kyra rose out of the water, her mother witnessed a peaceful glow on her face.

That day Kyra gave her church a picture of death to self and resurrection to new life. The old had gone the new had come. Kyra's new walk of faith would last another twenty-one years.

5

The Move to Cartersville

The Big Move

Kyra knew something was up when she saw her mom and dad talking quietly at the kitchen table. Her discernment was confirmed the next day when Joe called her in from playing in the yard. The beautiful summer day made it hard for Kyra to give up her playtime, but she ran to her daddy when she saw the look on his face as he stood in the doorway.

Joe led Kyra to the kitchen table where Karen was sitting. He took a deep breath. "Kyra, I have taken a new job in Georgia. We will be moving to Cartersville, Georgia, in the next few weeks."

Kyra burst out, "What? We are moving?"

The idea of leaving her neighborhood, school, and church friends was a little overwhelming. She did not know anything about Georgia. She had never even heard of Cartersville. Kyra hung her head, and her pig tails bounced forward. The best way she knew to handle this life interruption was to ask questions. Would there be new friends waiting for her in Cartersville? Would she have her own bedroom? Could she decorate her room any way she wanted to?

Karen and Joe did their best to answer Kyra's questions without making any promises. They had questions of their own, and both struggled with moving their family of five to another state.

Kyra said goodbye to her Tennessee friends and began looking forward to her new beginnings in Georgia. She had a lot of thoughts as her family began packing up boxes for the move. What would her new house look like? Where would she go to school? How would she make new friends? She would be starting the fourth grade in a few weeks. Who would be her fourth-grade teacher?

It was not long before the new house on Old Alabama Road in Cartersville, Georgia, was transformed into a home with the sounds of three little girls playing with their toys, sister squabbles, and laughter at family game nights. Karen worked quickly to get the girls enrolled in the Cartersville school system. As Kyra walked beside her mom during their tour of Cartersville Elementary, she thought, *These halls are so much wider than my other school. Everything is purple. I like purple.*

Meeting the Neighbors

Little did Kyra know that a few houses away from hers, another little girl was also looking forward to fourth grade.

Carreth Pendley did a double take as she and her family drove past Kyra's house. The house had been vacant for a while. Now three girls were playing in the front yard!

"Momma, did you know we have new neighbors? Can we go meet them?"

Melody, Carreth's mother, had already seen the cars with the Tennessee license plates. "Yes, of course. It looks like they have a daughter around your age."

A few days later, in the hot August weather, Carreth and Melody walked over to meet the Carps. They rang the doorbell and immediately heard footsteps running through the house. Kyra peered through the peephole before opening the door with a big smile.

Melody asked, "Is your mom home?"

Kyra's smile grew even bigger. She turned her head and yelled, "Mom, we have company!"

That one knock opened the door to a solid friendship between the Pendleys and the Carps that is still strong to this day.

Tabernacle Baptist Church

One December afternoon, Karen stopped in the long carpool line to pick up Chelsey. Mrs. Hewlett, Chelsey's kindergarten teacher, poked her head through the door as she opened it for Chelsey. She cautiously asked Karen, "Would you and your family like free tickets to see the Living Christmas Tree?"

With questioning eyes, Karen responded, "A living what?"

Mrs. Hewlett explained, "It is one of Cartersville's most treasured Christmas events." She handed Karen a printed invitation.

When Karen got home, she put the invitation on the refrigerator.

Glad to see her mom, Kyra ran into the kitchen. "Hi, Mom, can I invite someone over to spend the night on Friday?"

Karen reached for the invitation and responded to Kyra. "We were invited to Tabernacle Baptist Church to see a singing Christmas tree."

Kyra looked confused. "A singing what?"

Karen looked at the invitation again. "Well, actually, it is called the Living Christmas Tree."

Kyra still looked a little puzzled, but this sounded like something she might enjoy. She was always ready for a new adventure. "Mom, I should probably wear my new black patent leather shoes."

"Absolutely." Karen was relieved that Kyra wanted to go.

Kyra walked away from her mom wondering, *Will I see any of my friends at this big tree thingy?*

On the anticipated night, Kyra heard the orchestra and the festive Christmas songs as her daddy parked their car. "Wow, Daddy, there sure are a lot of cars parked out here."

Excitement was in the air. Karen and Joe crossed the street with their three daughters bouncing beside them. Kyra's fancy shoes made a tapping sound as she skipped.

Kyra stood still for a moment when she spotted the fifty-foot Christmas tree in the sanctuary. The wooden frame shaped like a tree was covered with thousands of evergreen pieces, ornaments, and lights. She had never seen such big red, green, and gold ornaments! And there were people in the tree. They started singing Christmas songs.

"Joy to the World" was familiar to Kyra. She hummed along with the music. She was mesmerized by the twinkling glow around each singer's face. Kyra felt goosebumps as she listened to the last song of the night, "The Hallelujah Chorus."

Kyra did not see any familiar faces other than Chelsey's kindergarten teacher. But she was not disappointed. She loved being at this new church. She did not want to leave the beautifully decorated sanctuary that was full of joy and peace.

Karen and Kyra thanked Mrs. Hewlett for the invitation as they passed going out the door. The big tree held out the branch that pointed the family of five to their new church family. The Carps joined the Tabernacle Church family at the beginning of 1994.

6

Kyra's Friendships

Gifted at Friendship

*I*f anyone knew how to make friends, it was Kyra. She was gifted with a high emotional intelligence in that she could find common ground with anyone she met. She valued people and knew how to have both deep conversation and light talks.

The following anecdotes from three of Kyra's friends represent lasting friendships from her childhood and teen years.

Carreth

"Mom, you are pulling my ponytail too tight!" Kyra complained as she prepared for the middle-school sock hop.

"I am sorry, Kyra, but if you want to look like you live in the fifties, we have to pull your hair high."

She called out to Joe, "Daddy, come look at me." Kyra shook her ponytail from side to side as she swirled into the

[handwritten marginalia: fascimile / Electrician / who committed / Suicide?]

living room. Her poodle skirt flew around her. Black and white saddle shoes and white ankle socks completed her outfit.

Just as Kyra asked, "Mom, when is Carreth's mom going to pick me up?" she heard the distinct sound of the maroon antique 1960 MG Midget convertible pull into the driveway. Kyra and Carreth impatiently posed as their parents took pictures.

Finally, they got in the car and were more than elated to be driven to the sock hop in the convertible with the top down.

There was one small challenge—the classic car would not go backward!

What in the world? Joe thought as he helped Carreth's mom push the little car out of the driveway where it would face Old Alabama Road. *Are they being driven in a car that will not go in reverse?* Of course, the girls did not care. They just wanted to make sure their friends saw them as they arrived at the dance.

When Kyra felt the merciless wind during the drive to the middle school, she was glad her ponytail was tight.

The girls arrived in timely style as Elvis Presley was belting out "Hound Dog." They hopped out of the car and bounced into the dance.

Then Melody sighed and looked for a nearby parent to help her back up the MG.

> Kyra for me was a friend that would point me to Jesus. She was the best listener and encourager. She had an adventurous spirit and was always full of new ideas. No matter what was going on in her life, she would ask me how she could pray for me. Her life was a life of reaching others and telling them about her Savior.
>
> ~ Carreth Pendley

Laura

Laura saw the new girl walk into the fourth-grade Sunday school classroom. She had been attending Tabernacle Baptist Church since she was three years old and knew the importance of being kind and reaching out to new people. Laura went over to Kyra and introduced herself. "Hi, I am Laura."

Kyra, being friendly herself, accepted Laura's kindness. Later, she informed Laura, "I am the oldest of three girls."

"Well, I am the *youngest* of three girls," Laura answered.

Laura asked where Kyra went to school.

Kyra replied, "I go to Cartersville Elementary. Where do you go?"

Laura told her that she lived in the county and went to White Elementary.

Although Kyra had no idea what a county was, she did know she liked Laura.

The girls would see each other practically every Sunday through their senior year of high school. Laura ate lunch with the Carps on many Sundays. Karen and Joe got used to hearing the bands Jimmy Eat World or Incubus playing on Kyra's CD player on warm Sunday afternoons. They would look outside to see Kyra and Laura in their bathing suits laying out on beach towels on the concrete driveway. The girls were oblivious to what was going on in the surrounding world.

Kyra and Laura were opposite in many ways. Kyra was blonde; Laura was brunette. Kyra went with the flow; Laura was a planner and strict rule follower. Their common ground was their shared desire to love God and others.

One Sunday as Kyra and Laura talked, their conversation shifted to prayer.

"I really want to be better disciplined at praying for others," Laura shared.

Kyra looked at Laura, thinking, *I am not the organized one in this friendship, but I can tell her what I do.*

Kyra showed Laura her prayer journal. She explained how she divided her friends and family and assigned them to days of the week. Each day she would look at her list and pray for the people listed on that day.

These two friends shared childhood enjoyments as well—mission trip experiences, young love stories, wedding bliss, and young motherhood.

> I have learned many things from Kyra. One of the greatest things I have learned is how to demonstrate God's love for others at every turn. Kyra demonstrated grace, compassion, and selflessness consistently. She was one of the most thoughtful persons I have ever known. Her hospitality was endless.
>
> ~ Laura Glaze McCoy

Anne

Tenth grade was a pivotal year for Anne Culverhouse. She had transferred to Cartersville High and had her eye out for new friends. It did not take long for Anne to notice Kyra. Or was it Kyra who noticed Anne? As she took note of who belonged in the many typical high-school groups, Anne observed that Kyra was friends with everyone, yet she marched to the beat of her own drum.

One day at lunch, Kyra spontaneously looked over at her friend and asked, "Anne, would you like to go to church with me? All the tenth-grade girls meet at 9:30 on Sunday mornings. I know that is a little early, but the time spent there is worth it. Our leaders are awesome." Kyra said all this without taking a breath.

Anne thought to herself, *Kyra is consistently the same with everyone. Maybe I should say yes to going to church with her.*

The next Sunday, Anne relaxed a little as Carreth Pendley and a few other girls she knew walked into the room where the girls their age met. She immediately related to Alexis Vance and Cindy Walker, Kyra's Sunday school leaders. All she could process was *They are so nice.*

After a few Sundays of attending the Sunday school and worship services at Tabernacle Baptist, Anne knew that she wanted to make a public statement of her new faith. Her conversation with Kyra started out with, "I think I want to be baptized. Isn't that how you let the church know that you have made a decision to follow Jesus? I have thought about it a lot."

Kyra tried to contain her joy as she guided Anne to talk to Brother Steve, their youth pastor.

When Kyra watched Anne walk into the baptismal pool, she cheered inside. *This is so cool! Thank you, God.*

Anne confidently told Brother Steve, "Yes, I place my faith in Jesus Christ."

The whole church clapped as Anne came up from the water. Kyra glanced over at Anne's parents. She was not sure what they were thinking, but she knew this was an important moment. It was not long before the whole Culverhouse family decided to join Tabernacle.

Anne and Kyra's friendship extended beyond school and beyond church. They were always at each other's homes. They brought out the best in each other. On New Year's Eve 2000, Anne asked Kyra to spend the night. With the year 1999 ending and the new millennium beginning, the girls had no worries as they listened to classic rock and chomped down on veggies, dip, and chocolate chip cookies. Their laughter and deep conversations shut out the loud firecrackers exploding in the subdivision next door.

What a better way to enter a new year than with a friend who totally accepts you yet also challenges you to be the best you?

> Kyra was my best friend for a time in my life. I loved her deeply. She was like a sister to me, and her family was my family. She was hysterical, and she thought I was funny too. She called me out when I needed it, even when it hurt. She was always there for me. I would do anything to talk to her now.
>
> ~ Anne Culverhouse Sheffield

7

Kyra's First Mission Trip

The Beginning of Kyra's Love for Missions

It was before sunrise when the two Greyhound buses, one Hertz moving truck, and one church van pulled out of the church parking lot. The parking lot was filled with families who'd come to say goodbye to the eighty youth and twenty adults headed to Marshall, Minnesota. Kyra was going on her first mission trip! For the last three years she had been hearing about her youth pastor, Brother Steve, taking students on mission trips. Now she would finally get to see for herself exactly what a mission trip was.

Steve McCombs, affectionately known as Brother Steve, began serving as the youth pastor for Tabernacle Baptist Church in 1994. His passion to see young people have a personal and growing relationship with Jesus Christ stood out to the many families he served. One of Steve's strengths was his commitment to challenging young people to prepare their hearts and minds for service. The preparation process began in January, months before the mission trip in June, when they started their Passport project. This Passport included Bible study assignments, sermon notes from regular church attendance, ministry team practice meetings, and Bible verse memorization. As a recent graduate of the sixth grade, Kyra had eagerly completed her Passport assignments. She couldn't wait to get started on the service part of the mission trip she'd heard so much about.

"You Can't Make It Tough Enough for Me to Complain"

The trip from Cartersville to Marshall took twenty-seven hours. The kids and adults resisted every urge to be grumpy on the long trip. Brother Steve had pounded a motto into each "missionary" in the caravan: "You can't make it tough enough for me to complain." The close quarters and long ride put this statement to the test.

When the team finally arrived in Marshall to set up backyard Bible clubs, they faced another test: figuring out how to put a positive spin on the very large mosquitoes that greeted them.

After arriving on Saturday evening, the teams began to unload the packed vehicles. The moving van was full of all the supplies needed for the backyard Bible clubs, as well as the drama, puppet, and clown teams. It took quite a while to get all the sound equipment, crafts, clown outfits, makeup, puppets, snacks, drinks, and one hundred suitcases to the correct destinations!

Brother Steve's hard work was about to pay off. Each backyard Bible club team was responsible for building relationships with children through playing games, telling Bible stories, and creating crafts. The teams were spread out over the city of Marshall, so as many children as possible could hear the message of Jesus. Marshall was considered a pioneer mission area, which meant there were few churches. At twelve years of age, Kyra got to see the importance of church planting in areas where churches were scarce.

Tornado Watch

On Saturday night, the exhausted mission team rested in the Southwest Minnesota State University dorms. Their first event was a choir concert Sunday afternoon at the sponsoring church. They proved that not only could the Tabernacle youth operate puppets, dress as clowns, and act in the drama team, but they could also sing. Kyra and her fellow students had prepared songs from the musical *Light Brigade*. Some of the favorites were "We Are the Overcomers" and "The Battle is the Lord's." They also had an ensemble that would sing separately.

The team was well prepared for the mission even when they faced a couple of hiccups along the way. The first mishap came when the group arrived at the sponsoring church and discovered that, due to some staff changes and lack of communication, the church didn't know they were coming. As if that wasn't enough of a challenge, when the team was about to leave for the church on Sunday afternoon, they found out that a tornado had been spotted close by, prompting a tornado warning. This was not a big deal for the locals, who lived in Tornado Alley. For Kyra and the rest of the Georgia folks, however, this was an emergency!

Brother Steve called the church leaders to tell them the situation. They responded, "It will be okay. We can still have the concert."

Brother Steve thought a moment and said, "I think we will wait until the storm passes."

The group did make it to the church but only had time to present a puppet show. Kyra served on the puppet team. She held her Eliza puppet straight over her head and above the curtain for all to see. Eliza threw back her big blonde head and sang like there was no tomorrow! Through Eliza, Kyra could communicate jokes, stories, and songs that held the attention of both children and adults. Even at twelve, Kyra's arm was strong enough to hold up Eliza while moving the puppet's mouth and arms. "Ticklish Reuben" and "The Do Right Family" made the reserved Minnesota audience laugh out loud.

Kyra Gives Away Her First Bible

Kyra and her fellow team members spent Monday through Thursday mornings with the children at the backyard Bible clubs. The clubs were held in parks or church members' backyards. They held evenings block parties around the Lyon County communities, providing the young missionaries opportunities to sing, share their testimonies (their stories), present dramas, and do clown and puppet ministry. The teams would set up a puppet curtain, a sound system, and a grill at a local park or neighborhood cul-de-sac. While the cooking team grilled hot dogs and hamburgers, the other teams interacted with the guests. It was a great opportunity to listen to their stories and to share the love of Christ.

During one activity, Kyra met a six-year-old boy. He was especially drawn to her and the puppets. While listening to the little boy, Kyra realized he did not have a Bible to call his own. Kyra looked at the Bible that she had gotten when she was six and decided it was time to hand it over to this first grader. The little boy grinned big enough to show he was missing his top front teeth. I wonder if he ever realized just how neat it was to have a Bible signed by the legendary Adrian Rogers!

Laura Glaze looked at Kyra after she gave the Bible to the little boy and thought to herself, *What in the world is Kyra going to do without a Bible for the rest of the trip?* Laura's second thought was, *Kyra's mom is going to be so mad that Kyra gave that Bible away!* Laura was always amazed by the way Kyra could just roll with the moment. Perhaps their opposite temperaments were what drew Laura and Kyra together to be best of friends.

Karen was a little taken back when Kyra told her about the Bible staying in Minnesota, but she was also proud of Kyra's act of love.

Mission trips do have a way of bonding the teammates, as everyone works together for a common goal. The singers, the actors, the puppeteers, and the clowns all played a role in bringing the message of Christ's love to a church and community that needed a dose of encouragement and hope. And Kyra got to be part of it.

Flip-Flops from the Mall of America

On the last day of the trip, Brother Steve and team loaded up all the equipment and missionaries to begin the trek back to Cartersville. The caravan began traveling east on Highway 19, 127 miles to Bloomington, Minnesota, where the Mall of America resides. Everyone had three hours of free time to enjoy at the mall before meeting back at the food court to load up and travel home.

Three hours was just enough time for Kyra to head to Bloomingdales to browse through the sales. She squealed as she spotted a pair of purple and lavender striped flip-flops on the sale table. Not only were the flip-flops her size and style, but they were also from Bloomingdales! Kyra loved to buy things at a discount price from expensive stores. With the flip-flops in her bag, she headed to see the wonders at Lego Land and ride some of the rollercoasters in the middle of the mall. Brother Steve always made sure the youth mission trips had a day of fun, and the mall day was exactly that!

The Welcome Home

As the caravan got closer to Exit 288 off I75-S, the mission team could see balloons and "Welcome Home" signs on the exit bridge. The parents and other church members made sure the group knew how much they had been missed. The youth heard loud cheering as they exited the buses in the church parking lot. Joe, Karen, Chelsey, and Sydney were there to welcome Kyra. Kyra talked about her Minnesota adventure the whole way home. "I can't wait until my next mission trip!"

8

A New Home

Kyra's Dream Room

"This is a dream come true," exclaimed Kyra as her dad gave her the tour of the home that would soon be theirs. "My own bedroom *and* my own bathroom!" She felt a little overwhelmed over this potential promotion in her life.

The small bathroom she shared with her sisters on Old Alabama Road would soon be a memory. The new had come. The old had gone. No more crowding of all her essential bath products and cosmetics. No more tension or telling her sisters, "That is mine. Leave it alone."

Kyra watched as the last moving van pulled out of the driveway on Old Alabama and headed toward her new home on Ardmore Circle, just a few miles away. Although the family's new location was closer to her school and church, it was a change and that would require some adjustment.

When her friends opened the front door at her new split-level home, Kyra would shout, "I'm down here!" This reminded them that visiting her now required traveling south on the steps down to the basement. Kyra's new beginning in "down under" provided an opportunity for her to use her creative, decorative juices. It started with a fun shopping trip to Bed Bath and Beyond. Karen and Kyra left the store with a buggy full of pink bedroom paraphernalia.

Painting the Bathroom Party

Kyra's bathroom was just around the corner from her bedroom. Decorating the bathroom took some fortitude and patience. It was a place of refuge for Kyra. The fragrance of lavender soap often traveled up the stairs as Kyra relaxed in her bubble-filled tub. She would close her eyes and chill out as soft music played and candles flickered. Bubble baths were her favorite way to relax, so it was important that her bathroom atmosphere be peaceful yet cheerful.

One Saturday morning, she was sitting on her pink bed aimlessly looking in her closet. Her eyes were pulled toward the striped platform flip-flops lying on the closet floor. As Kyra reminisced about her purchase from her first Tabernacle youth mission trip to Minnesota, sparklers went off in her brain. Her mind was bursting with creativity. She imagined how her bathroom would look with the same lavender and purple stripes.

Kyra thought, *This is it! I can use a two-by-four and a pencil to draw stripes on the bathroom wall. Oh, and I can invite my friends to come help me paint. A paint party!*

With the help of Joe and a trip to Home Depot, Kyra purchased the paint and paintbrushes. She set a date for the paint party.

She started with her friend Heather. "Can you come over on Thursday after school to help me paint my bathroom?"

With a puzzled look, Heather responded, "Sure, what time?"

"Come around five."

Kyra went in search of Melody next.

When Heather and Melody met up later, they planned the logistics for how to get a ride to Kyra's bathroom painting party.

Kyra readied the pencil, the two-by-four, and painting supplies. She gathered the food, greeted her friends, and opened the garage door for ventilation. The last step was to turn on the CD player. Relaxing baths called for soft music, but painting parties called for loud tunes. It was a warm evening when the team began drawing the stripes and applying the paint. Kyra instructed her friends to paint one stripe lavender and the next stripe purple.

The stripes were a great picture of Kyra's ingenious mind as well as her love for friends, fellowship, and fun.

Kyra's kick-off paint party just happened to be the same night as the Widows Banquet at Tabernacle Baptist Church. Joe and Karen had attended the banquet and were looking forward to a quiet evening at home after a long day away. They had no idea what awaited them when they drove into the driveway. Instead of a quiet house, they were welcomed by loud music, the smell of paint, and boisterous laughter. *What in the world?* They wore expressions well practiced by parents the world over.

It is true that even in the best of families, members forget to share plans with each other. Karen and Joe had known about the painting but not about the party. The paint aroma hit the surprised parents the moment they entered the basement. Treading lightly, they walked down the hall to see the newly drawn stripes, a few painted ones, and a few of the floor tiles freckled with purple dots.

Karen and Joe caught their breath, calmly communicated with Kyra that the painting party was bad timing—the next day twelve high-school senior boys would be invading her basement space for Disciple Now Weekend. Wide-eyed, Kyra and her friends rushed to hide all the painting tools until they could arrange the next painting party.

Disciple Now Weekend

Disciple Now Weekend was an annual outreach event led by Tabernacle Baptist youth pastor Steve McCombs. Around 150 middle-school and high-school students were divided into groups according to their grades and genders and gathered in homes on Friday and Saturday. After evening worship services at the church, each group was bused to their assigned home with a trained college student to lead them. Disciple Now was a time set aside for teens to experience a spiritual awakening. It provided an opportunity for young people to find community and support and to learn that God's ways are always better than human ways. Every student would have an opportunity to embrace God's extended hand of love and grace.

The twelfth-grade guys assigned to the Carps enjoyed staying in the basement. They probably did not even notice the half painted striped bathroom, or at least they didn't mention it. After a good meal and devotions, they wrestled, tossed a football, and enjoyed playing jokes on each other.

Kyra did not mind lending her space to the guys for the weekend. She was enjoying her own Disciple Now at the Vance's cozy cottage. Disciple Now weekends were special to Kyra all through her middle- and high-school years. Spending two nights with thirteen of her favorite friends was always a treat.

When Kyra came back home on Sunday afternoon, a new scent welcomed her—the sweaty smell from guy's wrestling combined with fresh paint. After eating lunch and giving her family a faint smile, Kyra headed down to her space. It did not matter at that moment what her room smelled like. She fell into her bed from exhaustion and slept the rest of the afternoon. She woke up around 6:00 p.m. just in time for an overdue bubble bath in her half-painted bathroom.

> I remember going to visit the Carps as a little girl with my mom. The room that stood out the most was Kyra's purple and lavender striped bathroom. I asked my mom if she would please let me paint our bathroom with stripes.
> ~ McKenzie Vance Hawkins

9

Eat, Beach, Sleep, and Repeat

High-School Breaks

"Wah, wah, wah, wah!" Mrs. Smith seemed to be speaking in Charlie Brown fashion as her voice pulled Kyra out of her daydream back into the classroom. Kyra stared blankly at her teacher's moving mouth hoping she had not missed anything important. When the bell rang to signal one class closer to her trip to the beach, the freshman grabbed the note she had written and dashed out of the classroom. She plopped the note into Heather's hand when they passed in the hall. Heather nodded, smiled, and opened the note.

> *Two more days until spring break! Pack all your bikinis so we can swap. We will be on the beach sunrise to sundown to eat, beach, and repeat! Ask Melody to pack her radio. Sleep over at my house Friday night so we can leave early Saturday!*

Saturday finally arrived. Joe filled up the van with gas before loading up Karen, Chelsey, Sydney, Kyra, Melody, and Heather. Each brought their own pillow, blanket, and snacks. Like most practical dads, Joe tried to make a rule about restroom stops, but good luck with that!

As Joe drove, the girls sang along to hip-hop on V103. Listening to the chatter and singing behind her, Karen looked over at Joe with a loving smile. She was silently communicating her thankfulness for his patience to drive the rowdy crew to Florida.

Nine hours later, as the van pulled up in front of the white trailer, Joe's mother, Lois Carp, fondly known as G-Lo, came outside to meet her son and family. Kyra jumped out to hug her grandmother. The smell of bacon rushed out of the front door when Kyra, Melody, and Heather dragged their luggage inside. G-Lo made them feel welcome with her famous bacon, lettuce, and tomato sandwiches and potato salad. After enjoying the meal, the whole family walked the ten-minute journey to the beautiful Fort Myers Beach. A gorgeous sunset provided a great beginning to a week on the beach.

Every night Kyra and her friends looked at the weather forecast, praying that rain would hold off until after they left for home. Then they planned which bikinis to wear the next day. They were all the same size, so they could interchange the twenty bikini sets that they had between them. Beach shoes were a little different as Heather and Melody wore a size six and Kyra wore an eight.

The bright morning Florida sunshine invited the girls to stay all day on the beach. Karen watched as the three beach bums walked away from the trailer. They looked like Charlie's Angels, walking in sync while wearing their sunglasses with their beach towels across their shoulders.

The girls felt the warmth of the sun on their faces as they walked across the arched bridge. Their hair flew in the salty wind while cars whizzed by on the other side of the pedestrian walk. Kyra liked walking to the beach because she could stop at the top of the bridge to take in the scenery of Estero Island. She breathed in the breathtaking beauty of the endless blue water. They passed the 7-Eleven convenience store on the right as they headed toward the water. Every day they would make a trip or two to the 7-Eleven for their favorite Slurpees.

At the end of each day, the trio trekked back over the bridge to G-Lo's. They looked forward to the snacks that she always had waiting for them. Laughter filled the trailer as the bathing beauties took turns showering off all the suntan lotions and oils. The water pressure felt so good in the block shower that was built into the enclosed patio. The green plastic fake grass at the bottom of the shower oozed through their toes.

The close of spring break came way too quickly. Early Saturday morning, Joe petitioned everyone to get in the van. It was time to go home. The girls slowly dragged their belongings to the back of the van. G-Lo exchanged hugs and goodbyes. She stood at the door watching her loved ones pack up.

As long as she held her grandmother in view, Kyra continued to wave out the window to G-Lo. She was already thinking of their next beach trip. The girls slept almost the whole drive back to Georgia. Joe didn't mind at all. It meant fewer stops along the way.

"What a great week," Joe said as he looked in the rearview mirror at his sleeping suntanned daughters and friends.

The beach beauties enjoyed a few more spring break trips to G-Lo's before high-school graduation. Later when Kyra got her first college schedule, she quickly checked for the spring break dates and contacted her grandmother. She asked her college friends Christi and Katie to mark their calendars.

Spring Break College Style

Kyra, Katie, and Christi felt the nudge to do more than just lay on the beach for spring break at G-Lo's. Night life was a big attraction as well, along with shopping for fun shoes. Kyra could build an incredible outfit around a strong pair of high heels. After being in swimsuits with no makeup all week, the idea of dressing up, fixing their hair, and putting on mascara and lip gloss sounded inviting!

During their night on the town, the college girls entered Cantina Laredo, a popular Mexican restaurant. Kyra couldn't help noticing that heads immediately turned. Going out, looking gorgeous, and getting attention from strangers made her and her friends feel beautiful. However, Kyra felt uncomfortable at the same time.

Before charging out of the restaurant into the world of night life, Kyra lovingly suggested to her friends that they return to G-Lo's little white trailer. In her diplomatic style, Kyra convinced Katie and Christi to play games and watch movies for the rest of the evening. G-Lo popped some of her delicious popcorn as she listened to their chatter.

These seasons of spending a week at the beach ended the spring before Kyra got married. But she held on to the wonderful memories of fun at G-Lo's. She would never forget her grandmother's famous BLTs, the shower with fake grass, and the walks across the bridge. No more listening to Cash Money Millionaires, Q-Tip, Tweet, and her other favorite bands on the beach—at least not during spring breaks.

> Kyra would always say, "Besides God and family, the only reason for living is spring break."
> ~ Heather Short

10

Cars, Cupcakes, Concerts, and the Cozy Cottage

Rhonda Honda

*K*yra looked at the picture on her newly acquired driver's license. *This could use some work*, she thought. *Do I really look like that?*

She was so elated over passing her driving test that she gave the picture a pass. She proudly placed the coveted piece of plastic into her wallet. One of the first among her friends to get a license, Kyra was also one of the first to get a car.

Joe had been searching for the right car for Kyra for a while. It had to be reliable and in the realm of his budgeted amount.

The whole family waited in anticipation to see Kyra's response over the new 1989 silver Honda.

Kyra did not disappoint. She squealed and exclaimed over and over again, "Thank you, Mama and Daddy. Thank you so much."

She gave her sisters a ride around the neighborhood. Then she headed off to show the car to friends. Kyra affectionately named her car Rhonda Honda.

One of the things Kyra liked best about having her own car was being able to drive to school. She signed up for her parking spot at Cartersville High. Heather and Melody soon earned parking spots. Heather's gold Toyota was named the Golden Nugget and Melody's purple Ford Taurus was dubbed Crash due to the big dent in the back. All three friends now had their own rides.

One morning Kyra rushed out of the house to drive to school. When she opened the car door, she immediately sniffed the foul air. *What is that smell? What animal has been in here?* She was in a hurry, so she postponed the search for the root of the odor. She opened her window and hung her head out so she could breathe fresh air.

After school Kyra offered to take her friend Davis Sinyard to work. Davis got in the car. "Kyra, I don't mean to be rude, but what is that smell?"

"I am so sorry. I know it stinks. After I get you to work, I will investigate."

After dropping Davis off, Kyra, quickly drove home and into her driveway. She held her breath as she looked in the backseat. She saw something white and grainy on floor.

I don't remember buying any rice. She looked again. *Oh, no! The rice is moving!* Then she saw the plastic bag. *That is not rice.* The crawling specks were coming out of the bag, which held tomatoes from a trip to the store. *Ew! I forgot about the bag of tomatoes.*

Kyra almost gagged.

The bag of tomatoes had been in the car for nearly a week. She cleaned up the mess and sprayed the back floor with anything that would kill the germs and stench. Once

Kyra told her family and friends about the awful experience of housing the white grubs in her car, Rhonda Honda was fittingly rechristened the Maggot Mobile.

The newly named vehicle was still a favorite ride for Kyra and her friends. Aside from a lingering odor, the Honda did great.

Then came the evening when Kyra tried to roll up the driver's side window and it wouldn't budge.

"Come on window," Kyra said out loud. "It is late, and I am tired." The window would not go up. Exhausted after school and work, Kyra whispered a quick prayer as she entered her house. "God, please don't let it rain."

She was relieved to see a dry car the next morning. After buckling her seat belt, she cranked the car as she turned the radio to V103. Just as the radio DJ said, "Good morning," Kyra was greeted with a flying object from the back of her car.

"What in the world?" Kyra screamed and swatted at the flying creature. Her blonde hair flew around as she recognized and dodged a little bird. The poor thing seemed just as confused as she.

Kyra finally got her wits about her and exited the car. She spoke softly to the bird. "You'll have a much nicer life outside, trust me." After a little more coaxing, the bird finally flew out. Kyra got back in, drove out of the driveway, and headed to school.

She discovered that cold air can also be an issue in a car whose window will not roll up. In the frigid cold winter of January 2003, Kyra and Davis were driving home from Athens, Georgia, which took two hours. Any passing motorist on the highway who spotted the Maggot Mobile probably also noticed the green sleeping bag in the front seat with two heads of hair and two pairs of eyes sticking out of it. One shaking red hand held the steering wheel. Yes,

Kyra and her friend had laced the sleeping bag across them in hopes of staying somewhat warm during the two-hour drive back to Cartersville.

In her teen years, Kyra had the reputation of driving fast. Her heavy foot caught the attention of officers with blue lights on top of their cars on several occasions. A hidden policeman watched Kyra zoom by him one morning as she was headed to school. Kyra saw him pull out behind her and turn on his blue light. Taking a deep breath, she slowed down and steered over to the right side of the road. As she was stopping, her water bottle spilled over into her lap. The police officer seemed a little overwhelmed when he looked inside the car and saw that Kyra was completely wet around her waist and legs.

"Do you know why I pulled you over?"

Kyra sheepishly pointed to the wet area.

After an awkward moment of silence, the officer sent Kyra away with a warning. With a shy smile, she thanked the officer and let him assume what he wanted to. Despite Kyra's struggle with trying to get places quickly, her quick wit was something to be admired!

Agan's Bakery

Kyra often provided Davis with a ride to school or work. One afternoon after school, Kyra drove Davis to Agan's Bakery on Main Street. He had been working there since ninth grade. The owner of the bakery, Mr. Agan, had asked Davis if he had any friends who might make a good employee. Davis remembered this conversation when Kyra was dropping him off and asked her to come inside the bakery to meet Mr. Agan. Kyra went with the flow and went inside to meet Davis's boss. Mr. Agan did an informal interview and offered Kyra the job. She started the very next day, which was the beginning of her two-year career at Agan's Bakery.

Davis and Kyra enjoyed working together. Their work hours were filled with serving the customers and laughing at each other's jokes. Mr. Agan often gave them free bakery goods for their friends and family. Kyra embraced any opportunity to give away Agan's rolls and cupcakes.

Going to "the Mall"

When Kyra turned eighteen, she was ready for more adventure. She really enjoyed her home life, all her friends, school (which may have gotten a little old by her senior year), and her church life, but her life felt a little mundane. She was also figuring out how serious she was with her faith in Christ. Kyra wanted to do what would honor God. She was just trying to figure out what that meant.

Driving to concerts in downtown Atlanta was one way that Kyra safely spread her wings. The Masquerade venue in Atlanta had a sketchy reputation, but it was a great place for concerts. Kyra and her friends especially enjoyed the venue's eighties nights. Davis, Melody, Heather, and others joined Kyra for these concerts. It was not so much the concerts, like Britany Spears in the Toxic Tour, it was more about figuring out how to maneuver being eighteen. Like many parents of young adults, Joe and Karen didn't always know exactly where Kyra and her friends were driving when she claimed they were headed to "the mall."

For one eighties night, Heather drove the Golden Nugget down to the Masquerade music venue. As Kyra and Heather walked up to the entrance to show their IDs confirming they met the admission requirements, Heather realized she did not have her driver's license. When the two walked back to the Golden Nugget, it was locked! Heather called her brother and asked him to please put her extra car key under a flowerpot on the front porch of their home. Heather then called Melody and asked her to go to her house, retrieve the key from under the flowerpot, and then drive fifty miles to bring the key to her best friends. As Heather was talking to Melody, a kind homeless man entered the parking lot scene. Seeing that the friends were locked out of their automobile, he offered to open the door for $50. The man tried but unfortunately (or maybe fortunately) was unable to get the door open. An unhappy Melody eventually arrived in Crash. Melody had saved the day, but Kyra and Heather drove home from "the mall" without seeing that evening's concert. So much for eighties night.

The Handsome Guy in the Photo at the Cozy Cottage

Kyra and her church friends enjoyed going to the Vance's for the yearly Disciple Now weekends and for an occasional Saturday night sleepover. Every few months, Kyra and the Sunday school girls would remind their teacher, Alexis Vance, that it was time for a sleepover at her house.

The Vance's log cabin always smelled like vanilla-scented candles. Soft worship music played in the background. After spending the night, the whole group would ride to church together on Sunday mornings. But first came the fun of Saturday night. Kyra and her church friends ran around in the big yard, played with Alexis Vance's young daughters, visited their horse Jack, played games, and gobbled down Alexis's delicious food. After dinner, the girls would gather in the living room. While sitting on the white shag carpet, they listened to Alexis give an encouraging devotional.

During one visit, cross-legged Kyra was trying hard to focus on listening to Alexis. She'd gotten distracted by a new framed picture on the entrance table, which happened to be directly in Kyra's line of vision. The photo of the handsome young man was hard to ignore. Soon Kyra, in her entertaining way, had a few of the other girls looking at the picture.

Seeing the smiles and hearing the giggles, Alexis realized she had lost the attention of the girls. She explained, "That handsome guy you're looking at is my younger brother, Philip Reid Karr IV. He is a senior at UGA."

The girls were a little impressed with a name that ended with an IV, but they were also disheartened when they realized he was already in college.

Girls can dream though, right?

Fast forward to Kyra's senior year. She mentioned to Alexis Vance that she wanted to learn how to play the piano. Alexis smiled big and told Kyra that her mom, Janet Karr, was a great piano teacher. Even in her busy senior year, Kyra began going to Janet's house for lessons. One afternoon as Kyra was plunking on the piano, Janet's son Reid (that would be the very handsome Philip Reid Karr IV) stopped by his mom's house to pick up something. Janet rose from the chair next to Kyra to welcome her son with a hug. She then introduced Reid to Kyra.

Kyra, realizing that this handsome man was the one in the picture on Alexis's table, held her composure. With her bright smile she told Reid, "It is nice to meet you. I hear you attended UGA."

Reid said that he had recently graduated but was planning on returning to get his master's.

Kyra kept the conversation going. "I am planning on attending there. That is, if I get accepted."

"I hope you do get accepted. It's a great college. In fact, if you want, I can show you the ropes on campus."

"Thank you. That would be great."

As quickly as Reid had entered the room, he exited and

was out the door to his next meeting. He thought to himself, *She is really cute. Too bad she isn't a little older.*

11

2003: A Pivotal Year

High-School Graduation

*I*n 2003, football fans witnessed the underdog Tampa Bay Buccaneers beat the Oakland Raiders in Super Bowl XXXVII. The movie *Finding Nemo* debuted, and *Chicago* won the Oscar for Best Picture. Baseball fans watched the Florida Marlins beat the New York Yankees in the ninety-ninth World Series. In the science world, the Columbia space shuttle broke apart while reentering earth's atmosphere, killing the seven astronauts on board. George Walker Bush was our president. In March, our country joined Britain to declare war against Iraq. While all of this happened, Kyra was making the exciting shift from high school to adulthood.

Yes, a lot was happening around the world, yet in Cartersville, Georgia, the world seemed small as Kyra and almost two hundred other high-school seniors were about to receive their diplomas at Weinman Stadium.

On the evening of the big event, the Carp family was busy trying to get ready. Karen encouraged her family to hurry. "Come on everybody! We want to get a good seat so we can see Kyra up close."

Joe, Karen, Chelsey, and Sydney rushed out of the house after wolfing down chili dogs. They found a seat at the bleachers just as the "Pomp and Circumstance" processional began to play. Karen was teary eyed as the senior Hurricanes marched onto the field. Joe peered into the sea of purple and white gowns for his senior. *Where is she? I am pretty sure she will be close to the front since her last name begins with a C.* After a moment of searching, he spotted Kyra.

Dressed in her white graduation cap and gown, Kyra sat in her assigned seat on the football field. She looked around at her classmates. Then her eyes traveled to the bleachers. She wondered where her family was seated. She grinned when she thought she saw her daddy's blonde head in the crowd.

As the valedictorian and salutatorian made their speeches, it was hard for Kyra's mind not to wander.

Where has the time gone?

We have a great senior class.

Will I ever see my classmates after this?

Kyra looked at the crowd and spotted the attendance clerk, Linda Kellogg. *I will miss seeing Mrs. Kellogg. It was so fun working with her in the attendance office.*

She turned her attention to the teachers on the stage behind the speaker. *This may be the last time I see Mr. Foster. Melody and I sure made some memories in his class.*

She saw Coach Downer and remembered the fun she'd had playing softball. *I did not want to make a career of it, but I learned so much from her.*

Spotting Heather brought back memories of spring breaks at G-Lo's. *What would spring break look like from now on?*

I know things will be different.

How in the world am I going to be a college student in just two months? She prayed that she would make good decisions in college. She'd picked comparative literature as her major and Italian as her minor. Not everyone understood why she'd want to major in that, but she was excited.

Then she zeroed in on her friend Davis and smiled. *What will Agan's Bakery do without Davis and me?*

Kyra came back to the moment as the students in her row stood up. *This is it. I am about to graduate from high school!*

Even though the principal had asked everyone to please hold their applause to the end, it was just too hard for the Carps to keep quiet when Kyra's name was announced. She heard their cheers, "Go Kyra!" as she shook Principal Hamby's hand. She smiled at the photographer. It was such a surreal moment.

After Kyra and her friends turned their tassels, they tossed their caps into the air with raucous cheers as new graduates. Families and friends rushed onto the field. Kyra was smothered with hugs and kisses from those who knew her best and loved her most.

Kyra's Last Youth Mission Trip as a Student

The summer after Kyra graduated from high school, she went on a mission trip to Reno, Nevada. Brother Steve, his wife, Tonia, Kyra, Laura Glaze, Lauren Woodward, and Natalie and Brookeanna Jenkins made up the team committed to serve as volunteers at the Reno ESPN Great Outdoor Games. The seven volunteers looked for opportunities to share their passion for Jesus with the guests, athletes, and game administrators. The team also accepted an opportunity to work with a church in Reno. They stayed in the educational part of the small church. Sleeping on air mattresses and sharing a small bathroom didn't bother the friends at all. It was like a big slumber party.

Brother Steve usually had every meal and activity planned out during mission trips. If one did not like the chosen eatery, they smiled and ate there anyway. Imagine the surprise on Kyra's and her friends' faces when their leader offered them a choice of where to eat! They were dumbfounded and shocked and wondered if he was serious. But over the next few nights, what started out as a newfound freedom quickly turned into a pain. Meeting everyone's likes was a challenge.

One night they decided to eat at one of the casino buffets. Even though the meals were expensive, the girls agreed and went through the line to pay before they ate. Kyra was the last one in line. She paid for her meal, then thought about how much she'd spent. *I don't want to spend this much money for a huge amount of food. I know I won't eat that much.*

Kyra decided to ask for a refund. She politely told the team she would sit with them while they ate but planned to eat somewhere else. One teammate looked at Kyra, then at the lady at the register. She also quietly asked for a refund. A few minutes later, the whole team had left to find another restaurant with their refunds in hand. Kyra's nickname for the rest of the trip was Refund.

The hot weather did not hinder Kyra and the team from serving well. Before the week was over, many of the athletes and administrators knew them by name. Some of the team even went on stage to help present the medals. The girls gave out hundreds of bottles of water and shared their testimonies whenever they had the opportunity.

After the Games were over, ESPN treated all the volunteers to a night out at the Taj Mahal of Tenpins. This national bowling stadium is the only facility of its kind in the world. The seventy-eight championship bowling lanes provided plenty of opportunities for the ESPN staff and volunteers to have a grand time. Even with the loud music and noise of falling bowling ball pins, Kyra managed to hear her name called over the speaker. She had won a bowling ball! Not just any bowling ball, but a ball that smelled like black cherries. It was marbled with a black cherry color. Even when Kyra realized the ball was too large for her suitcase, she carried out her bowling ball with pride. She also carried it in her lap on the plane trip home.

Kyra sat by an older gentleman during the flight. He asked about the bowling ball in her lap. Kyra told him how she got it, which led to her sharing the mission behind the trip. His response was, "Oh, you are one of those." Then he proceeded to critically question Kyra about her faith. Kyra was able to lovingly and skillfully address each question the man asked. By the time the plane landed in Atlanta, the man told Kyra, "You have given me a lot to think about."

Brother Steve, who had overheard the conversation as he sat behind Kyra, smiled and said to himself, *I believe that Kyra just might have a calling on her life to missions.*

After the team returned to Cartersville, Kyra began the process of getting everything ready for her move to the University of Georgia in Athens.

12

The College Years

Kyra Goes to College

What a thrill to get accepted into the University of Georgia! In 2003, Kyra joined the ranks of 5,190 other freshman to begin the journey of figuring out young adulthood. She missed home, but Cartersville was less than two hours away. Kyra found comfort in having two of her best hometown friends, Davis and Heather, right across campus. She also began working at The Grind Coffee Shop in downtown Athens. Her busy schedule kept the homesick bug at bay.

Kyra chose to allow UGA to assign her first roommate. They placed her with a girl named Ashley. Ashley and Kyra met for the first time when they moved into the Creswell Dorm, the oldest dormitory on the UGA campus. At first Kyra was a little frustrated because she had her eyes on Russell Hall, which at that time was a newer and nicer dorm. It turned out that Kyra and Ashley had landed in the better dorm because each room had its own window air conditioner. Russell Hall dorm had central air, which stayed broken most of the time. Win for Kyra!

Comparative Literature and Italian

Initially laid-back Kyra was unsure of her major before deciding on comparative literature with an Italian minor.

Upon hearing Kyra's decision, Laura, one of her best friends since fourth grade, wanted to help Kyra understand the ramifications of this decision. "What on earth will you do with that?"

After a few seconds of reflection, Kyra shrugged. With a sweet smile, she replied, "I don't know. I like to read, and I like Italian, so maybe I will teach. Who knows? All I know is, I just really enjoy both."

Laura smiled back at Kyra, but inside she was thinking, *She is out of her mind! Why isn't this a bigger deal to her?* She had a much more practical plan in mind: mass communication and sociology.

Years later, when Kyra was a missionary in Italy, Laura visited her in Rome. "Kyra, you taught me more in that quick conversation about your college major than I learned in any of my college classes. After you prayed about your college major, you went with what you enjoyed. Now look. God was leading you the whole time!"

The way Kyra chose her college major was the way she responded to life. Kyra based her decisions on how God created her. She went with the way she was bent even though those closest to her may not have understood.

Meeting Katie

Christi and Lauren were from Marietta, Georgia, and lived across the hall from Kyra. Their close friend, Katie

Blair, also a Lassiter High School alumnus, often visited the two girls and became acquainted with Kyra. Whenever Katie visited her friends, she would see Kyra. It wasn't long before Katie and Kyra began a friendship that would stand through the thick and thin experiences of life.

The freedom of being away from home was exhilarating for Kyra and the other thousands of UGA freshmen who had invaded Athens.

One of the first things Kyra and her new friends did was to try out the nearby bars. Most of Kyra's friends decided to get fake IDs. Kyra vetoed that idea for herself but was willing to have an ID passed back to her so she could also enter the bars. After a few visits, however, Kyra told Katie, "The bar scene is just not for me. I don't want to do this anymore."

While Katie was still at the stage of wanting all the world had to offer, it became obvious that Kyra was going in a different direction. Even with this difference, the friendship was strengthened through times of reflection and deep conversations, lots of laughter, and getting involved in a growing college ministry.

A Well-Loved Cul-de-sac Nanny

In Kyra's quest to plug into a local church, she discovered Watkinsville First Baptist. The 123-year-old church, which had opened in 1880, was alive and vibrant and attracted many UGA students. Located on Simonton Bridge Road, about twelve minutes from Kyra's dorm, it was easily accessible. What really drew Kyra to the church was the Wednesday night Bible study for college women. The weekly study was led by the pastor's wife, Carla Sibley. Kyra enjoyed going to Pastor Carlos and Carla's home. Carla's hospitality and the connection with the other college co-eds made

Wednesday Kyra's favorite day of the week!

In order to prepare for the study on Wednesdays, Carla needed a college student to come two hours early to help her clean house and get everything ready. She asked Kyra, who immediately responded that she would.

Kyra started helping Carla every week and eventually became a nanny for her five children. Kyra had such a great reputation that she was soon helping three other families in Carla's cul-de-sac: the Tomlins, Smiths, and Greens. All the families agreed that they did not know what they would have done if Kyra hadn't helped them through that busy season of life.

One evening when Carla and Carlos were out for dinner, Kyra called in hysterics. "I am so sorry, Ms. Carla. I am just so sorry. I promise I only turned my back on Wilson for a few seconds. He's been beside me all night."

Carla asked, "Kyra, is everyone okay? Is anyone hurt?"

"No, ma'am. Everyone is fine, but your bedspread and bedroom are not. My roommate is looking up how to get black marker out of fabric and off walls."

Wilson was less than two years old. He'd decided to add a little flair to the white bedding, walls, and bedroom furniture.

"Don't worry, Kyra. The main thing is that everyone is safe. Thank you for calling me. We will be home shortly."

Kyra breathed a sigh of relief.

This potential disaster that had loomed in Kyra's mind became only one of many fond memories of the beloved cul-de-sac nanny.

Kyra was enjoying a busy life with her nannying, classes, Bible study group, and working at the coffee shop. She did not think she could make time for anything else. Until Reid Karr walked into The Grind.

Chemistry at the Coffee Shop

Reid was at UGA working on his master's in social sciences. He'd recently learned from his sister Alexis that Kyra was working at a coffee shop in Athens. When Alexis mentioned Kyra to him, he immediately thought of his friend David Drew.

Reid spent a lot of time with David. During one of their conversations, Reid looked at David like a lightbulb had just turned on in his mind. "David, I know a cute girl who works downtown at The Grind. I think I might be a little old for her. She is closer to your age. Do you want to go meet her?"

Knowing that Reid was a good judge of character, David agreed to go. If nothing else, he'd heard they had good coffee.

David and Reid parked the car and walked a few blocks, following the smell of coffee. As soon as they walked into The Grind, Reid spotted Kyra. It is fair to say that she eyed him at about the same time.

Kyra was behind the counter creating mocha drinks and greeting her coffee-loving customers with her bright smile. When she saw Reid, she immediately said hello to him. "It's really good to see you. How are you?"

Reid responded, "Hey, just thought I would drop by. This is my friend David."

Kyra greeted David with a grin from ear to ear. "We are slowing down a little, so let me ask my boss if I can take my break. We can sit over there by the window."

A few minutes later, Kyra joined her two visitors at the round table. Reid and David noticed how easy it was to talk to Kyra. She was comfortable talking about shallow things as well as deeper subjects. Reid was struck by her relaxed composure.

After Kyra's break, she excused herself to go greet new customers. Something happened in Reid as he watched Kyra walk away in her jeans, T-shirt, and black Converse tennis shoes. His first thought was how mature she was for her age. *Five years isn't too much of an age gap.*

Reid didn't have to explain anything to David. They were close enough that he knew what Reid was thinking. "Go for it," he told Reid.

As soon as those words were out of David's mouth, Reid's mental wheels began turning to plan the next time he could see Kyra.

Reid went back to The Grind a few days later. He invited Kyra to join him and some friends at the annual Athens Twilight Criterium. Kyra had heard about the famous cycle race and accepted the invitation. They joined thousands of other people who were also participating in the downtown festivities surrounding the race. It was exhilarating to watch hundreds of cyclists from all over the nation and world race through downtown Athens.

Reid watched Kyra as two bands—The Weight and Cracker—preformed at the Criterium celebration concert. Reid's mind was active with thoughts *What is different about her? Should I ask her for a date, just us alone?*

After a few more visits to the coffee shop, Reid asked Kyra to see a movie, *51 First Dates.*

Kyra did not have to think twice before accepting. She enjoyed the irony of realizing their first real date was to watch Adam Sandler and Drew Barrymore have their first date fifty-one times.

When Reid dropped her off at her apartment after the movie, Kyra ran to find Katie. "Katie! We had so much fun. Pinch me. Just pinch me. Is this really happening? Katie, I am not looking for a boyfriend."

Katie was so tickled for her friend. "Just go with the flow, Kyra. See where it goes."

Kyra tried to relax and not worry about Reid. She was sure that he would call her again, but it was hard to be patient. She jumped with joy the second she saw Reid's name show up on her cell phone. Of course, she gained her composure before answering his call with a warm, "Hey, Reid."

"Hey, Kyra. I was just wondering if you have ever seen the laser show at Stone Mountain?"

"Yes, but it has been a while." Even if she'd just gone yesterday, she would say yes to Reid!

Reid continued, "My sister Robin and her husband invited us to go this Saturday. Would you like to go?"

"I would love to."

Robin and Curt met Reid and Kyra at Stone Mountain Park. The blanket they brought to sit on fit perfectly on the grass among the thousands of other people who'd come to watch the laser show and listen to the great music. They snacked on chicken strips and chips as they watched the children and adults play frisbee and catch around them. The sun went down, and the moon came up. The warm weather was perfect as the lasers blasted the side of the mountain. It was an incredible show of lights moving in rhythm to Ray Charles singing "Georgia on My Mind." I am sure that Reid was on Kyra's mind much more than Georgia.

The couple became very close as they continued to spend time together. Somehow between their classes and work, they managed to build a strong friendship.

13

Dreams Come True in 2006

Weaving Dreams

*T*ime has a way of weaving dreams into stories, stories into history, and history into legacy. For Kyra, time wove little-girl dreams into her big-girl world in 2006. In the sixth year of the new century, Kyra's life took on a whirlwind of experiences.

The year began with Kyra's college football team playing in the 72nd Sugar Bowl. Atlanta's Georgia Dome was packed with over 74,000 football fans on January 2, 2006. The crowd was loud, and the stands of the dome were saturated with the red and black colors of the Dawgs. (The Sugar Bowl was normally held in New Orleans but made the change to Atlanta due to the aftermath of Hurricane Katrina in 2005.) Unfortunately, the favored Bulldogs lost to the West Virginia Mountaineers, 38 to 35. Still, it was an exciting way to kick off a senior year.

Where had the time gone? As she walked the halls of the

Franklin Building, Kyra could not believe she was beginning her last year at UGA. While reminiscing, she walked past a flyer tacked to a bulletin board. She saw the bold letters that read "May Semester in Budapest." A picture of ornate European buildings with beautiful snowcapped mountains in the background grabbed Kyra's attention. To top it off, visiting Italy was on the trip agenda! The pull in her heart to go was solidified when her anthropology professor announced the trip in his classroom. Kyra couldn't wait to ask her parents about the possibilities of studying abroad.

Kyra approached Karen and Joe with a convincing speech. "Going to Budapest would be such a great opportunity. Not only will I earn college credits, but I can practice my Italian in Italy. My college minor will finally be useful!"

Joe and Karen responded with the look that she had received throughout her life—the look that said, "We want to support you, but are you sure?" They recognized that this was another creative idea that Kyra had set her heart on. Even though this would be her last summer at home before graduating from college, they wanted Kyra to chase her dreams.

Kyra ran the idea by Reid. She knew that being separated from Reid for any amount of time would be hard. She also knew that Reid had plans to work all summer at a dude ranch in Idaho. Both Kyra and Reid agreed that time apart for the summer would be a good opportunity to gain clarity about their relationship and their future.

Once Kyra's family was on board, she invited her roommate Christi to jump on the study abroad train. Kyra urged Christi to seize this once-in-a-lifetime opportunity. After all, when would she have another chance to travel, have fun, and earn college credits at the same time? Christi wondered how the trip could contribute to her exercise science degree, but she agreed to go to the informational meeting. Assured that her major did not matter for this course and that she could even earn college credits toward her degree, Christi started to warm up to the idea. When the meeting for committed students was held at Professor Bendek's home, Kyra and Christi were both in attendance.

College Senior Abroad

After completing the first semester of classes on campus, Kyra and Christi, along with eighteen other students and a middle-aged professor, headed to Budapest. The excited group gathered at the Atlanta airport on May 15. Fourteen hours later, after a layover in New York City, they finally landed in Budapest.

The Central European University Center in Budapest would be Kyra's home base for the May semester. The dorms were small, but each student had his or her own room and bathroom. The goal of studying abroad was to encourage the students to use their voice to express their point of view. Kyra was able to participate in many discussions about different cultures, ideas of government, education, and religion.

As Kyra walked around Budapest with her "buddy" Christi (each student had a buddy for safety), they heard music from America's Top 40 in every store they visited. Kyra soon discovered that her favorite part of Budapest was the Danube. She was amazed at the magnificent river that ran 1,777 miles through ten countries. Beginning in the Black Forest of Germany and flowing into the Black Sea of Romania, this mighty river struck an emotional chord in Kyra. After seeing the Danube, she journaled, "Koszonom God for this experience. May I bless your name (Psalm 103:1) with my life and actions." *Koszonom* is the Hungarian word for "thank you."

After being in Budapest for several days, the students

embraced a new friend—their bus driver, Maricash. Maricash drove the students to ten other countries outside of Hungary. Kyra made great strides to record these visits. But there were days all she could get out was "My head is spinning" or "I feel like I am in a dream." Her most common statements were "I miss Reid so much!" and "I got to talk to Reid tonight!"

When the students visited Italy, Kyra got to converse in Italian with a little boy and his mom. It was the highlight of her time there, outside of visiting the Colosseum. The most difficult, and the only time she expressed sadness on the trip (besides over missing Reid and her family), was when the group visited Geneva, Switzerland. The Swiss landscape was breathtaking, but Kyra was distracted by a woman she saw hanging out at a brothel near where she and her friends were eating lunch. Kyra expressed her sadness in her journal. Her response did not flow from judgement or criticism but a concern for those trapped in prostitution. How many girls were there because they'd been forced into that lifestyle? How many wanted their freedom? It made her all the more thankful for the blessed life she got to enjoy, but the experience burdened Kyra. The compassion she felt for the women paved the way for her future work in Rome.

Mission Trip to Rome

After almost two months of European travel, informative discussions, and good times, Kyra's study abroad ended. However, her time in Europe would last another six weeks.

When Kyra registered for the study abroad trip, she also signed up for a short-term mission trip to Italy. She figured since she was already in the vicinity, why not stay five weeks longer to serve in Rome and Naples? She was assigned to help develop an outreach strategy in Rome to reach 250,000 university students with the gospel. This was a perfect time to practice her Italian as she listened and talked to hundreds of people her age.

On her first full day in Rome, Kyra toured the Vatican and Saint Peter's Basilica. The bright sunshine and heat bore down on her as she waited behind approximately two hundred people to enter the Vatican Museum. Seeing Michelangelo's Sistine Chapel was worth the wait and the sweat. Kyra eventually tired of the heat, but on this first day she journaled, "It is ridiculously hot here, but for me it adds to the magic."

Kyra not only worked with the university students, but she also served the missionary families in any way she could, hoping to encourage them in their ministry journey.

Kyra spent the last three weeks of her summer serving a small Baptist church in Naples. She coordinated with the International Mission Board strategist to lead two English ministry groups that had come to serve in Naples as well. Her main job was to help with the language barrier. This was her first experience of translating Italian for the English-speaking guests. Her time of serving in Italy gave her a deep love for the Italian people.

Italy Wins the World Cup

Outside of the mission work and delicious fresh Italian food, including the daily treat of gelato, the best thing she got to experience was being in Italy when they won the 2006 World Cup against France. *Italian Campioni 2006!* The game was played in Germany, but that did not stop the Italians from gathering in Rome to hear the outcome of the game.

What a night! There were over 200,000 people at Circo Massimo, and after Italy won, it was complete and utter chaos. We walked around in the parade of people for a while. I almost got hit with a firecracker!

~ Kyra's Journal while in Italy

Kyra's stay in Rome ended on August 1, 2006. She headed home eager to go see Reid in Idaho at the end of August.

A Surprise Visit from Reid

"Let's see how we feel after our summer separation." That was the gist of a conversation that Kyra and Reid had in the spring of 2006. While Kyra was in Europe and Reid was in Idaho working at a dude ranch, Reid made an important decision.

He did not want to be separated from Kyra.

Reid knew that the litmus test for marriage was when two individuals were apart and knew for certain that they didn't want to live apart. He wanted to marry Kyra and commit his life fully to her.

Kyra had just returned home from her summer spent abroad, but Reid still had a few weeks left to work at the dude ranch. Kyra had no idea that the separation would come to an end sooner than expected.

A gifted strategic planner, Reid began carrying out the best procedures to get the marriage train on the tracks. His first step was to ask Joe for Kyra's hand in marriage. Reid asked Joe to pick him up from the Atlanta airport but to keep this visit to Cartersville a secret from Kyra.

Joe met him as requested. After exchanging warm greetings, Reid told Joe of his intentions to eventually attend

Southern Seminary. After a pause he said, "I am wondering if you would mind if Kyra went with me."

Thinking that Reid meant just for a visit, Joe said, "Oh, sure. She can meet you there for a weekend."

Reid realized he was going to have to be a little clearer. "I want to marry Kyra."

Not surprised, Joe responded, "Oh, Karen and I suspected that you might be coming to talk to us about that."

As they drove the thirty minutes to Marietta, the two men talked about how Reid and Kyra met, their dating years, and the future possibilities. Joe smiled inwardly, knowing he would soon welcome a son into his family of daughters.

Joe dropped Reid off at his mom's house and went back to Ardmore Circle with a big secret that he could only share with Karen. After a few hours, Reid arrived at the Carp home to surprise Kyra. He quietly entered the home as Joe and Karen each gave him a knowing smile. Reid crept down the stairs to Kyra's room. Her squeal could be heard clear to the other side of the cul-de-sac!

The two thoroughly enjoyed their reunion during the surprise weekend visit. Reid had a calculated plan that he had mapped out. The next step would take place in Idaho.

A Diamond at the Rocky Mountain Dude Ranch

What better place to get engaged, Reid thought, than the beautiful Saw Tooth Mountains of Idaho? He had worked all summer at the Rocky Mountain Dude Ranch and wanted to share the views with Kyra.

The Rocky Mountain Ranch covers nine hundred acres of priceless land in the Sun Valley area of Stanley, Idaho. With a population of only one hundred people, Stanley is noteworthy for its coffee brewing, fly-fishing, and extreme fluctuation in temperatures. Stanley's nickname is Trailhead to Idaho Adventure.

Reid invited Kyra, his sister Stacy, and her husband Ashley to visit him at the ranch. He was eager to introduce them to the beautiful place where he had worked all summer and show off his fly-fishing skills. Fly-fishing was a new hobby he had learned to really enjoy. Since the visit took place during the heat of August, Stacy struggled with the decision to accept the invitation. As everyone knew, she was not a camper. She thought of the heat and other potential camping hazards yet still decided to go because, after all, it was Reid. She could not turn down her older brother's special request.

Once his guests had safely arrived, it was time for Reid to carry out the next part of his pop-the-question plan. Reid loaded everyone up in the Jeep and headed to an area in the Sawtooth Mountains. After they arrived at the trail head, everyone put on their backpacks and hiked for two hours to Reid's special spot. Setting up camp in the heat was no easy task. After everything was organized, Reid asked Kyra to go for a hike. That was when he asked her to be his wife.

A short while later, Reid and Kyra walked back to the main camp—or more like skipped back. At least Kyra seemed to be skipping. She had just accepted Reid's marriage proposal.

Kyra left the Saw Tooth Mountains with an engagement ring on her left hand. She looked at it during the whole flight home. The only thing she wanted to accomplish before getting married was to complete her college degree. She received her degree on December 4, 2006, after three and a half years at UGA. Ten days later, on December 14, 2006, in a starlit outdoor wedding, Kyra said, "I do."

14

The Gift of Marriage

Juggling College and Planning a Wedding

Kyra was tempted to drop her Italian minor during her last semester. She called her mentor, Carla Sibling. "I cannot do this and plan a wedding."

Carla assured her, "Yes, you can."

And she did! Kyra stayed faithful to her studies and became a successful Bulldog graduate.

One tool that Kyra used to escape the academic pressures was to daydream about becoming Mrs. Reid Karr. Like many brides-to-be, she would take a blank piece of paper and write her upcoming new name over and over. *Kyra Karr. Kyra Karr. Kyra Karr.*

Kyra was often asked why she planned an evening wedding outdoors in December. She offered an understanding smile and never wavered from her desire for an outdoor wedding on that Thursday evening in December.

I remember congratulating Kyra when we met in the stairwell at Tabernacle. Her eyes were bright as she announced the date, time, and place.

"A December night wedding will be magical," I responded. "What are sweaters and coats for anyway?"

Joe watched the ten-day weather report. He wanted to make sure they wouldn't have bad weather for Kyra's wedding. Joe also counted every RSVP that came through the mail. It became a little humorous for the family to watch Daddy Joe calculate the cost for each card marked "Yes, will attend."

The weather was freezing one week before the wedding. But Kyra and Reid's big day dawned warm and sunny. Karen called Ray at Grand Oaks and canceled the hot chocolate and hot apple cider.

Ray told her, "Oh, honey, I have already canceled it. It is so warm."

The Big Day

I held a brunch for Kyra, Karen, Janet, and the bridesmaids at my home on the morning of December 14. After we'd filled ourselves with quiche, fruit, and muffins, Kyra gave each friend a round compact mirror decorated on the outside with colored rhinestones. The mirrors were made by a nonprofit organization to help women get out of unwanted difficult situations. This was a typical gesture for Kyra. There was jovial laughter around the table as the girls talked about their friendships and all the changes that the future would bring. As Kyra sincerely thanked everyone for sharing in her special time, I distinctly remember thinking, *Kyra is certainly one calm bride.*

The wedding felt like a true celebration. The white miniature lights illuminated the venue and transformed it into a winter wonderland. The ushers greeted the guests at the gate to the garden. There were seventy-five chairs on either side of the aisle. My heart fluttered with anticipation as I looked at the white arbor lights at the end of the garden aisle. Kim Lewis and I sat quietly beside each other and prepared our hearts for Kyra's special moment.

As the clock struck 6:00 p.m., Pastor Steve McCombs, Reid, and his brother Jared entered the garden from the right side while music played. The bridesmaids and groomsmen came down the center aisle, preparing the way for Kyra. The bridesmaids each carried white hydrangeas that beautifully accented their brown silk spaghetti-strapped dresses. The groomsmen looked sharp in their black tuxedos with brown vests and bowties.

Dressed in his black and white tux, Joe took a deep breath and extended his left arm to his daughter. Kyra wore a straight white strapless wedding dress of pure raw silk without decor. The simple silk looked elegant and stunning on Kyra. Her simple makeup and lip gloss topped off her glow. She wore a handmade, floor-length veil bordered with old fashioned lace tucked in at the top of her low bun.

Joe's eyes glistened as his firstborn daughter looked at him.

"Thank you for being a wonderful daddy," she somehow managed to say.

Holding her white hydrangeas bouquet in her left hand, Kyra slipped her right arm into the cusp of her daddy's left arm. Joe walked her through the twinkling lit arbor and down the aisle to meet Reid. Kyra glowed as she caught the eyes of her groom. After Joe was seated, a beautiful clear voice sang "Turn Your Eyes Upon Jesus." Lindy Cooper and her guitar touched all of our hearts as she sang Reid's dad's favorite hymn.

I truly had chills. Then, as I witnessed the couple exchange their convenant vows, I gazed up at the star-filled night. Yes, indeed, the night was magical.

After the ceremony, family and friends gathered at Grand Oaks in Cartersville (an antebellum home near downtown Cartersville) to eat dinner together and celebrate the covenant of marriage of two amazing young people. The smell of Ray Thacker's southern cooking added to the atmosphere of warmth and hospitality. Since neither Reid nor Kyra liked wedding cake, they served delicious cheesecake. The room resonated with laughter as the guests enjoyed the fellowship and food.

At the end of the celebration, Reid and Kyra ran through a tunnel of sizzling sparklers held by their guests. A 1938 black Buick convertible waited for them. Kyra's parents had rented the classic car from Ray.

The couple jumped into the car to rousing cheers only to find that it would not crank. The men of the wedding party immediately tried pushing the car in an attempt to jump the clutch. The car was dead. Curt McNiff, Reid's brother-in-law, piled the bride and groom into the front seat of his car, because he didn't have seats in the back. He drove Mr. and Mrs. Reid Karr away from the cheering crowd to the Carp's house, where Reid's car was parked.

After changing clothes, they excitedly got in the car to head off to their honeymoon haven in Atlanta. It was at that moment that Reid realized he did not have his wallet, so they spent the first hour of their marriage in a frantic search for it. After retrieving the wallet, which had fallen out in Jared's truck, they realized they were hungry. McDonalds was the only thing open, so they pulled into the drive-thru to order their first meal as a married couple before heading to their hotel near the airport.

The next morning their flight to Mexico was delayed, and their luggage traveled on a different flight. Finally, they landed in Cancun without their luggage, but their week was redeemed through beautiful sunsets, sandy beaches, and delicious Caribbean cuisine.

After a study abroad summer, an amazing Idaho marriage proposal, a difficult final college semester, and a wonderful Caribbean honeymoon, Kyra was ready to say goodbye to 2006 and settle in Watkinsville, Georgia, near UGA as Mrs. Philip Reid Karr IV.

Southern Seminary, Louisville, Kentucky

After nine months of Reid serving as youth pastor at Watkinsville Baptist Church and Kyra working as a nanny for several families in the Sibley's cul-de-sac, the young couple made the move to Southern Seminary in Louisville, Kentucky. The same day Reid began his theology classes, Kyra started working in their apartment, Village Manor Apartments, management office. Reid worked at the seminary gym where he met seminary student Steven Chambers. Steven recalls, "I was single and 450 miles away from home, so I jumped at Reid's invitation to visit his home. I admit the fact that Reid and Kyra had cable to watch college football enticed me to visit them, but soon they were like family. Kyra's warm hospitality and great cooking kept me going back week after week."

It was during their season in Louisville that they started discussing the idea of full-time ministry abroad. Before Reid graduated with his master's in theology, they applied to the Southern Baptist International Mission Board, which the missionaries refer to as "The Company." They were asked to list their three top picks of places to serve, and Rome was at the top of their list.

The application process for this type of career requires a lot of paperwork and multiple evaluations, so Reid and Kyra had to wait several months for confirmation that Rome would be their destination.

At about the same time they received verification that they would be headed to Rome, Kyra and Reid both stared at a positive pregnancy test. It wouldn't just be the two of them moving across the ocean.

15

A New Life in Italy

The Move to Italy

*K*yra sat on the couch in her small living room as she did every morning. All set with her coffee and Bible, she asked God to give her wisdom on what to take, store, or give away. She stared at all the belongings that she and Reid had acquired in almost three years of marriage. Most everything they owned, outside of furniture, was in piles in the living room, kitchen, and hallway. *How do I know what I am going to need in Rome? What am I holding on to that I really need to give away?* She considered the moving money allotted to her and Reid through The Company. Many of her wedding gifts would have to be left behind, as well as some of her favorite keepsakes.

One piece of advice that Karen gave Kyra was to be sure to pack something for her new home that would make her happy. For Kyra that meant little trinkets for her kitchen, her aprons, and a beautiful fragranced candle for her new bathroom.

After they decided what to transport to Rome, Reid and Kyra focused on their goodbyes to family and friends. They started with the good friends they had made at the seminary. Then they attended intense mission training in Virginia for a few weeks before their last set of goodbyes to their many loved ones in Athens and Cartersville.

Both Kyra and Reid's families knew that it would be two years before they could return to Georgia for a visit. For Karen and Joe, their only grandchild was moving five thousand miles away.

Karen shared a Bible verse with Kyra after learning of the couple's assignment to Rome. Kyra recorded the verse in her journal, revealing that when a family is called to take their love for the gospel of Jesus to a foreign land, it affects the extended family. Each member must figure out how to release their loved one to God's plan. Karen chose a Bible verse to show her support for her daughter.

> *Those who go out weeping, carrying seed to sow, will return with songs of joy, carrying sheaves with them. (Psalm 126:6)*
>
> *Mama called and shared this verse with me today. She will be sad when we leave, and so will we, but we know the seeds sown for the gospel of Christ will bring greater joy. Praise God from whom all blessings flow!*
>
> *~ Kyra's Journal*

Settling In

Kyra and Reid's first apartment in Italy was in San Paolo. It was a perfect location for walking to food markets, coffee bars, and the metro station. There was just one challenge . . . the apartment had mold. With their limited money for rent, it was difficult to find another apartment, but their persistence paid off, and they soon moved away from that moldy place.

Their second apartment was also in San Paolo, just blocks away from Basilica of St. Paul and minutes away from their favorite coffee bar, The Orange Bar. The fourth floor, two-bedroom apartment was just right for the Karrs. Kyra placed her aprons and happy trinkets in the small kitchen and her lavender scented candle in the bathroom.

Reid and Kyra used their budgeted money to buy a used vehicle. The car was helpful for taking trips not covered by metro service. Due to the lack of parking places in the city, they kept the car in their apartment's underground lot most of the time. It was easier to walk everywhere, plus moving around the city on foot was the best way to get to know the neighbors and community. They racked up a lot of steps every day on the crowded sidewalks.

Kyra and Reid found immediate community with the other missionaries. They had many prayer meetings and planning sessions with their fellow missionaries. Kyra and Reid both attended language school, since their first assignment was to make sure they could clearly communicate with the Italians. Kyra was already fluent, and Reid was a fast learner.

Along with learning the language, they had to learn the personalities and needs of the rest of their mission team. They dove headfirst into meeting neighbors, local merchants, and retailers.

Leonardo and Valeria De Chirico

Soon after moving to Rome, Reid and Kyra met Leonardo and Valeria De Chirico, a couple who had also recently moved to the ancient city. The couple was a bit older than Kyra and Reid. In 1995 when Leonardo was studying theology in Wales, Kyra was turning eleven. Reid was sixteen and had just lost his dad to a brain tumor. As Reid and Kyra continued growing up in Georgia, Leonardo and Valeria planted a church in Ferrara, Italy, and were involved in theological training in Padova. The two couples met in Rome in 2009.

Leo's love for history and for the gospel, as well as his training and experience, provided the perfect combination for beginning an evangelical church in Rome. He went right to the heart of the city, which hadn't had an evangelical church for a hundred years. They did not have a building, so the new congregation of Breccia de Roma rented the Waldensian Church basement just blocks away from the Trevi Fountain and around the corner from the Roman Forum.

Leo and Valeria invited Reid and Kyra to their home to discuss the future of church planting in Italy. Knowing that it takes a lifetime of commitment, the Karrs told the De Chirico's that they were on board. The two couples desired to plant churches where people could experience life based on the grace of Jesus. Pastor Leo, Valeria, Kyra, and Reid became very close friends as well as ministry partners.

Three Daughters

When I visited Kyra's home in Italy, I admired three beautifully framed maps on the wall in her dining room and living room area. The first map was of Indiana, the map in the middle was of Rome, and the third map was of Georgia. At first, I thought, *Oh cool, Kyra likes maps.* It took me a minute to realize that each map represented something important to Kyra. The wall hangings were more than just maps. They represented significant events that impacted Reid and Kyra.

Jeffersonville, Indiana
March 16, 2009
Nolyn Lynn

When Kyra found out that she was expecting her first child, she journaled her excitement:

> *I found out I was pregnant yesterday! Praise the Lord! Thank you for this blessing. Give Reid and me wisdom, O Lord.*

As Kyra approached her due date, the doctor told her the baby was breech. She went to a nearby pool to swim in hopes of getting her little one to change positions. She wanted to have an all-natural birth. Nolyn, however, liked her position and did not budge.

Reid called Karen and Joe early in the afternoon of March 16 to tell them that he was taking Kyra to the hospital in Jeffersonville, Indiana, for an emergency C-section. Jeffersonville was just across the Ohio River from their home in Kentucky.

Karen and Joe made plans to leave for Indiana the next morning at 6:00 a.m.

Close to midnight, Karen received the sweetest call from Kyra.

"Mom, she is here!"

Karen nudged Joe as she listened to her firstborn tell her about the amazing experience of seeing her own firstborn. "She is so perfect and beautiful. I cannot believe I am a mother." The morning could not come fast enough for the new grandparents.

A few days later, Kyra and Reid buckled up newborn Nolyn in her car seat and drove back across the Ohio River to their home in Louisville, Kentucky. Nolyn lived at the seminary apartments for only a short time before the family packed up and headed for Rome.

Rome, Italy
December 1, 2010
Ellie Drew

Boy, this was a big surprise! A wonderful surprise I might add. When I saw the test, I started laughing—I was so excited! Thank you, Lord, for your blessings! May this baby bring glory to your name.
~ Kyra's Journal entry in April 2010

During the first few weeks of her second pregnancy, Kyra was afraid she had miscarried. It was during this scare that she wrote in her journal:

I know from experience that pregnancy will draw me closer to you. I pray you would change me into the person you want me to be.

Ellie was born at Bambino Gesu Hospital in Rome on December 1, 2010. She had jaundice, which meant mom and daughter had to stay longer so Ellie could be under doctor's care. Kyra thought the Italian hospital food was delicious compared to American hospital food. She spoke to the nurses with loud, deliberate hand gestures, conversing like a true

Italian. She wondered about her seemingly erratic responses. What was wrong with her? Her midwife assured her not to worry. "Crazy hormones produce unusual behavior."

Kyra held Ellie close as they were finally released from the hospital. She knew that she was about to face not just the sleepless nights of a newborn but also the high energy of a toddler. Nolyn welcomed her baby sister, and they all adjusted to becoming a family of four.

Cartersville, Georgia
February 2, 2013
Livia Reid

At the end of 2012, Reid, Kyra, and the girls came to the states for a few months. Kyra was seven months pregnant with her third child and came under the care of Cartersville OB/GYN.

Kyra was busy with many responsibilities during this season. Her journal entries were few and far between.

> *Taking my glucose tolerance test. Thank you, Lord, for good medical care, a healthy baby, a car, a loving father to Nolyn and Ellie, friends to go see in Athens, family that eagerly welcomed us back home.*
> ~ Kyra's Journal, December 5, 2013
> *(Her first mention of a baby.)*

The next time Kyra mentions her pregnancy was January 8 when she penned this prayer:

> *O Lord, may I wait for your power and not try to rely on my own strength. I know this is the only way to bear fruit in my life. Teach me by your great mercy and love. I pray for*

Nolyn's school, Ellie's soft heart to be turned toward you at an early age, and for the new baby to bring much glory to your name, even before it is capable of making actions.

Kyra did not mention the name of the baby because she and Reid had decided to be surprised at the birth of all their babies. They did not know if this third child would give Nolyn and Ellie a sister or a brother.

On February 12, 2013, Kyra wrote:

Thank you, Lord, for my sweet Livia! What grace! What a blessing! May her life bring you great glory, may she know you, may I point her to Jesus.

I was able to visit Kyra a few weeks after Livia's birth. She honestly did not look like she'd just had a third baby. She carried Livia in a front baby pouch carrier as she welcomed me to meet her third daughter.

When Livia was three weeks old, Kyra and Reid invited friends Matt and Katie Smith to a concert in Atlanta. Katie, who was expecting her first child, asked Kyra, "Did you forget the diaper bag? What about a stroller? A pacifier?"

Kyra replied, "I have an extra diaper, and I folded a onesie in my wallet. Really, Katie, extra accessories and information books are nice, but all a baby needs are a drawer to sleep in and a mama to keep it fed and warm."

Kyra left a lot of stress behind with all the baby paraphernalia. After a fun night, baby Livia snuggled up against her mama, and Katie went home feeling the freedom and confidence to live without new-mom anxiety.

At one month old, Livia flew home to Rome with her mama, who kept her warm and fed, her two sisters, and her daddy. The Karrs were now a family of five.

Karen, Joe and newborn Kyra

Three-year-old Kyra

Reid and Kyra engagement

Kyra, UGA Graduate

Kyra at her Wedding

Chelsey, Karen, Kyra and Sydney

Kyra and Nolyn cooking

Chelsey, Joe, Sydney and Kyra

Kyra reading the Bible

Livia, Ellie and Nolyn under the sign
honoring Kyra at Breccia Di Roma
Church, Rome, Italy

16

Integrating Family and Work Overseas

A Family Overseas

As Kyra carried Livia off the plane in Rome, she watched her other two little girls walk ahead with their daddy. Back to the Italian friends who had become family. Back to the everyday surrender of wishing their American family lived closer. Back to rolling up her sleeves to cross the borders of language and culture. And back to the most important thing: building a foundation of trust with the Italians so she could point them to the One who was truly worthy of their trust.

After Livia was born, Kyra had to evaluate her roller coaster of feelings. She was completely committed to her work in Rome. Yet it sure had been nice being near family during Livia's birth and for a few weeks afterward. It was one thing to serve as a couple overseas; it took on a whole new meaning when little ones were added to the mix. Kyra knew that schooling for her girls would be different in Rome. She knew it would take extra energy for her and Reid to intentionally speak Italian in their home. As she reflected on leaving her American family and friends, she once again took her feelings and put them in the envelope of commitment. She asked her family and friends to pray for her and her family. It was indeed home. But it looked so much different than her comfort zone in Cartersville.

The Roles of Mommy and Missionary

Kyra relished her roles of wife, mother, and missionary. The position that kept her the busiest was, of course, motherhood. She knew that the time and energy she put into her daughters' development was her main responsibility. In making her home a priority, she supported Reid as he worked outside the home, building relationships with their fellow missionaries and Italian neighbors. She knew there was no ministry without authentic relationships.

This line of thinking did not fit into the Roman culture. Women were expected to work outside the home. Kyra knew this, yet as much as she wanted to build relationships in the community, her greater desire was to be fully committed to motherhood. She prayed that God would give her opportunities to build relationships while she cared for her family.

Meeting Helena and Pablo

Kyra got plenty of exercise as she and the girls walked to their various destinations. Daily walks to the sidewalk vegetable stands, grocery store, parks, and Nolyn's half-day preschool kept Kyra busy and in shape.

Nolyn quickly became friends with her classmate Pablo, which naturally led to Kyra having conversations with Pablo's mom, Helena. As their friendship grew, Helena noticed how gracefully Kyra responded to the challenges of life, especially the loneliness and difficulties of raising three girls in a foreign country.

One day at their favorite park, as the children played around a young olive tree, Helena asked Kyra about her values and beliefs. Helena recalled, "In her eyes there was a special light when she told me about her faith. I realized then how much Christ meant to her." It was at that moment that Helena felt a deep desire to come back to the Lord she had learned about as a child.

Then later, at a play date at the Karrs, Helena remembered, "As soon as I put my foot into the apartment, it was as if I could clearly hear Jesus's welcoming words. I imagine now that the way I felt was how the prodigal son of the Bible felt seeing his father's open arms. Now I understand that I was witnessing the fruit of the Spirit in Kyra—love, joy, peace, patience, goodness, kindness, faithfulness, meekness, and self-control." Through Helena's friendship, Kyra witnessed the answer to her prayers—knowing how to be a full-time mommy and missionary at the same time.

Bridging the Gap

One of the many challenges that Kyra faced while living in Rome was missing out on all the fun family activities in Georgia. She lived too far away for weekly get togethers, birthday celebrations, or impromptu visits. Although Kyra and her family and friends made good use of their electronic devices to converse through video, it was just not the same as being together in person.

When Kyra realized that her baby sister was about to experience a dream come true—a marriage proposal—she could not stand the thought of not being part of it.

Living up to her big sister reputation of being bossy, she took Sydney's engagement experience into her own hands.

Kyra's Surprise Plan for Sydney

"What? Mom, there is no way that Sydney can get engaged and me not be there! I will already have to miss all the wedding showers. I don't want to miss the engagement too. Daniel is just going to have to come here to Rome to propose to Sydney!"

With her big winsome smile, Kyra FaceTimed Daniel to convince him how awesome it would be to propose to Sydney in a picturesque setting in Rome, Italy.

Daniel Shadle and Sydney had been dating since 2009, so Daniel had been a part of the Carp crew for a few years. Knowing that Kyra was the brains behind most of the fun shenanigans for her friends and family, Daniel agreed to follow Kyra's lead. After all, it did sound romantic to get engaged in Italy. If nothing else, it would be a great story to tell their children!

Because tickets from Atlanta to Rome were not cheap, Daniel, a poor college student, knew he would have to start saving as soon as possible. He asked his parents, Laurie and Bryan, to give him money at Christmas and on his birthday to put toward the surprise proposal trip. Daniel made flight arrangements and planned to surprise Sydney while she was visiting Reid and Kyra in December of 2013.

Sydney and McKenzie Vance, Reid's niece, arrived in Rome early after an overnight flight from Atlanta to Rome. Reid picked up the exhausted girls and took them to the Karr apartment in San Paolo. Nolyn, Ellie, and Livia squealed as they ran to embrace their aunt and cousin. The Welcome Sydney and McKenzie sign made the moment even more special. They gathered around the table to enjoy the snacks Kyra had prepared to welcome the treasured guests. There was one little requirement that Reid and Kyra made clear:

the Georgians would have to stay awake until time for bed. That would be the only way to get used to the seven-hour time change.

To make staying awake a little easier, McKenzie and Sydney walked with Kyra to see the famous St. Paul Basilica located right there in St. Paolo. The magnificent cathedral, one of four of its kind in Rome, was built over the burial spot of Saint Paul of the Bible. The sleepy girls enjoyed seeing ancient artifacts but were thrilled to go back to the apartment in time for Kyra's delicious home-cooked Italian carbonara and chocolate tiramisu. After gorging themselves on the authentic Italian food, the girls were finally given permission to crash, and crash they did.

McKenzie and Sydney toured many famous sights that first week, from the famous Roman Colosseum to the Trevi Fountain. They even spent the night in Naples while visiting another missionary family. Christmas lights and decorations made everything feel festive and full of life. What a great time to be in Italy!

By the beginning of the second week, Kyra worried that Sydney might have seen or heard some of the secret plans and conversations. Daniel, also a little nervous about the secret getting out, mentioned to Sydney that he couldn't wait to see her when she returned from Rome and to plan on just the two of them for Christmas Eve evening. Having no idea at all what was about to happen, Sydney just took all the conversations in stride.

The awaited time had come for Kyra, Reid, and Daniel's surprise plan to be put into action. Daniel's flight from Atlanta landed on Monday morning, December 16. Sydney and McKenzie were sleeping in after a late night at church.

Kyra got them up earlier than expected. "Good morning! We have so much to do today. Let's get an early start."

Reid explained that he had to go pick up a pastor friend from the airport in Rome. Taking friends and fellow missionaries Caleb Boothe and Jason Davis with him, Reid left for the airport.

Meanwhile McKenzie, Sydney, Kyra, and her three daughters all headed for the flea market. They had just arrived when Kyra's phone buzzed.

Kyra told the caller, "Oh, okay. Well, thank you very much." McKenzie glanced with confusion at Kyra when she abruptly urged them on toward another destination while repeatedly looking at her cell.

Suddenly Kyra exclaimed, "Hey, let's get some breakfast. I'm a little hungry. How about y'all?" She steered the group to an Italian coffee bar.

Once seated, Ellie asked Sydney to take her to the restroom. When Sydney was out of sight, Kyra clued McKenzie in. "Daniel just landed at the airport. He is coming to propose to Sydney. I have had the hardest time keeping the secret, but now we can finally execute the plan."

Completely shocked, McKenzie smiled.

With McKenzie in on the secret, Kyra informed the group that they were now going to the Orange Garden, a beautiful yet simple park located on Aventine Hill in Rome. Built on Roman ruins and lined with spectacular Roman umbrella pines and orange trees, the park offered unmatched views of the city—a perfect place for a wedding proposal.

Meanwhile Reid, Jason, Caleb, and Daniel hid and covertly crept to the place where Daniel was going to pop the question. It was a beautiful morning, and the park had already filled up with locals and tourists. The four men hiding and creeping from tree to tree might have been a little suspicious, but no one pointed out their behavior.

Daniel finally reached the tree closest to the platform

overlooking Rome and Vatican City, with the gold dome of St. Peter's Basilica shining brightly in the sun.

Kyra gently guided the girls over to the platform, telling them that they just had to come see the view. McKenzie, Kyra, and Sydney were looking out over Rome when Sydney felt someone tapping her shoulder. When Sydney turned around, her face revealed the surprise that Daniel had hoped for.

Sensing the magic of the moment, McKenzie, Kyra, and even complete strangers backed away. Everyone watched the joy on Sydney's face as Daniel kneeled on bended knee.

Sydney and Daniel became engaged in the land that her big sister called home. It was a great day. Daniel was completely exhausted after going twenty-four hours without sleep, but he didn't care.

Back home in Cartersville, Georgia, the Carps and the Shadles rejoiced as they heard how the surprise proposal unfolded.

With Daniel by Sydney's side, the last week in Rome was a joyous time of sightseeing, celebration, and planning for the wedding, which would take place in Roswell, Georgia, the following summer. Of course, the wedding in Georgia was beautiful, but who can top a surprise proposal in Rome, Italy? Kyra Karr made it happen!

17

Holding the Rope

The Rope

*T*abernacle Baptist Church had committed to intentionally encourage the missionaries it supported. Service in a foreign country can be lonely and difficult. The spiritual battles are real. Steve McCombs transitioned from youth pastor to mission pastor before Reid and Kyra moved to Rome. Seeing the pressures that the Karrs and other Tabernacle missionaries were under, Steve knew that the church needed to step up and do its part in the Great Commission. He understood that while not everyone is called to serve in other parts of the world, all Christ followers are called to participate in the sharing of the gospel. Some go, all pray, and all give. Reid and Kyra were holding up one end of the rope in Rome, and the other end was being held by their brothers and sisters in Christ at Tabernacle.

Hold-the-Rope Vision Team

In September of 2013, Steve led a small prayer and vision team to Rome to visit Reid and Kyra. I joined Steve, along with Michael Gill and Laura and Spence McCoy. We were full of anticipation as we landed after the overnight flight. The goal was to gain a vision of the best way we could hold our end of the rope for the Karr family.

Reid picked us up from the airport around 7:30 a.m., and we hit the ground running. Our first stop was in San Paolo to meet Kyra and the girls. Once inside the apartment building, we rode the tiny half-door elevator to the fourth floor. I remember thinking, *I hope this thing doesn't collapse on us.* Before the door opened, I could hear small feet running around and little voices yelling, "They are here!"

Kyra opened the door holding Livia while Nolyn was peeking around her right side and Ellie around her left. Kyra was glad to see all of us, but Laura, her childhood friend, received the first and tightest hug. Since it was still morning, we walked with Kyra and the girls to drop Nolyn off at preschool. The weather was crisp and cool as Kyra carried baby Livia in her front carrier and rolled Ellie in the stroller. After dropping Nolyn off, we walked to the popular Orange Bar for coffee and delicious pastries.

My heart was so blessed as I witnessed the relationships that Reid and Kyra had built with the workers at the Orange Bar. Listening to their conversations, I could not translate a single Italian word, but I could understand the flow of friendly conversation. I sat there thinking, *This is so cool to be able to build relationships with people who communicate in a different language than your own.*

In that week I experienced life with an American family who had made Rome their home. I saw and felt the peace-filled home. I experienced, on a small level, the day-to-day struggles of integration into another culture.

I watched Kyra gracefully care for her family as she walked to the grocery store for fresh food and then prepared meals with equanimity and care while managing the needs of three active children. I listened as she spoke Italian to her neighbors and watched as she, like the nearby residents, hung her laundry on a clothesline that went out the window across her apartment courtyard.

Our days were full of connecting the ancient with the present. We rode the metro and walked at least five miles a day through the sights of Rome. I remember the awe I felt as I stepped out of the crowded metro to the immediate view of the 1,941-year-old Colosseum. When we stopped at the prison where the apostle Paul spent his last days, I paused with thanksgiving for the ways God used Paul's biblical epistles to help me understand how to grow as a Christ follower. We walked the streets while prayerfully asking God to open the hearts of the people to the grace of Jesus Christ. We prayed for all the missionaries as they battled the unseen forces of darkness. We asked God to save the lives of those who desperately need His salvation.

We met with Pastor Leo, Reid, and the other missionaries to plan and strategize ways that Tabernacle could best serve them as they worked day in and day out to build solid, loving relationships with the Italian people.

I was reminded that the missionary calling is not for the faint of heart. That is why we as a church knew we had to hold up our end of the rope by praying for them and sending teams to encourage them in their work. We left with the plan to send a serve team to Rome soon.

Hold-the-Rope Team Visit in 2015

In late May of 2015, Tabernacle Baptist sent a serving team to visit Reid and Kyra. When Joe Carp, Jeff Lewis, Parker Lewis, Pastor Don Hattaway, Nathan Hattaway, and Gary and Sherry Glaze landed in Rome, Reid was there to pick them up. Karen Carp joined the team a few days later after getting off work for the summer.

Kyra had a passion to reach out to the women in Rome who were victims of sex trafficking. Just as in the United States, this business is a huge money maker for the "businessmen" who control the bodies and souls of their "employees." Kyra, along with others in the ministry she volunteered with, was cautious but tried to be visible enough for any woman who was searching for freedom, encouragement, and answers. One evening, Kyra, Karen, and Sherry rode in a van through the streets with the volunteer ministry. The van parked in certain areas for the team to offer refreshments and a listening ear to any of the women who wanted to talk. The ladies were drawn to the pure love that Kyra and the team offered. Their experience with "love" was anything but pure. Indeed, the team was holding the rope with Kyra.

Reid invited the serving team to meet with small groups of Ethiopian and Sudanese refugees. Ministering beside the men of Breccia di Roma Church, the Tabernacle team helped to strengthen relationships through card games, refreshments, and shared personal testimonies.

As the team listened to Pastor Leo passionately communicate his heart for Rome, they learned a lot about Roman history and culture. His prayerful goal was to plant several churches in the city and surrounding areas through the main church, Breccia di Roma. While doing this great work,

Breccia di Roma's final hope was the transformation of the city of Rome according to the gospel.

The team also visited Breccia di Roma, which was housed in the rented basement of an older church building. The church may not have had a home of their own, but they had a powerful vision and a hope. While some of the team worshiped with Reid and the adults, the others helped Kyra in the children's church.

The team left Rome with a better understanding of the daily focus of missionary work. For Kyra it was the managing of motherhood and support for Reid, as well as making time for her Roman friends, fellow missionaries, and the outreach street ministry. For Reid it was building relationships in the community, working with The Company and Pastor Leo to plant churches, and serving his three daughters and his wife.

As a foreign missionary family, Reid and Kyra were encouraged when friends and family from home would come visit. They were especially encouraged when the 2015 serve team from Tabernacle joined them, though briefly, in the trenches of their work. The serve team was also encouraged, as they gained a better understanding of the vision of church planting and how to pray for their missionaries. The team left Rome knowing they were an extension of Reid and Kyra's work to fulfill the Great Commission.

The concept of holding the rope gives the clear picture that everyone can be a part of the Great Commission:

> Therefore go and make disciples of all nations, baptizing them in the name of the Father and of the Son and of the Holy Spirit, and teaching them to obey everything I have commanded you. And surely, I am with you always, to the very end of the age." (Matthew 28:19–20)

18

Summer of 2015

The Summer When Everything Changed

*I*n mid-June, not long after the Tabernacle serve team returned home, Reid, Kyra, and the girls used some vacation time to come stateside to visit. Outside of the quick trip to be a part of Daniel and Sydney's wedding the year before, it had been a couple of years since they visited the States. Karen and Joe's house was their home base, and they borrowed a vehicle from their friend Chris Sward to use during their eight-week stay.

They made time for people in Cartersville and Athens whom they had not seen in years. Kyra was able to visit many of her childhood, high-school, and college friends. Fun visits with Kyra and Reid's families were the icing on the cake.

Two days before they were scheduled to return to Italy, Kyra and her family sent a video to her good friend Damaris in

Rome to wish her a happy birthday. After receiving the video, Damaris thought, *I cannot believe they would take time while they are on vacation to think of me.* Kyra enjoyed being stateside but thoughts of her Rome family were always present.

After sending Damaris the video, Kyra visited Kim Lewis at Bartow Family Resources (BFR). She was so appreciative of BFR's ministry to women and their families. Kyra shared with Kim her desire to have a building for their church that belonged to them instead of using a rented space. Hoping to encourage Kyra, Kim shared the miraculous story of how BFR had attained their own building. Kyra looked past Kim as if trying to envision the dream in her mind and said, "I just don't know how that could ever happen to us." She said it with a longing and a hope that was compelling.

When Kim brought her down to my office, I looked up from my desk to see Kyra's bright smile. Jumping up, I tripped over my rug when trying to get to her. She laughed as I blurted out, "Some things never change, Kyra. I am still clumsy."

The three of us spent a few minutes talking about the work in Rome. We declared that God would do mighty things in Rome as we high fived Kyra and said goodbye.

The Text That Never Came

On the morning of August 14, 2015, Melody, Davis, and Heather awaited Kyra's text to let them know where to meet for breakfast. It was a last and long-awaited opportunity for the four friends, who'd known each other since their teen years, to gather before Kyra and her family returned to Italy. Each of the Four Musketeers (a nickname they had given themselves in high school) was looking forward to the reunion with Kyra while reminiscing over coffee.

Their shared memories were too many to count, although

a few stood out: Davis and Kyra working at Agan's Bakery; memories of their favorite teacher, Mr. Foster; crazy car stories; concerts; spring break adventures; and so much more.

As the morning passed without hearing from Kyra, they began to wonder if something was wrong. It was midmorning before they found out the news of Kyra's accident and death. The three pals, adored by Kyra, banded together to try to make sense of their friend's early homegoing.

The text did not come that morning. Neither did the laughter. Death had interrupted what seemed to be uninterruptable.

The Night Before

On the evening before the planned flight back to Rome, Kyra, Reid, their three daughters, and Kyra's family had dinner at La Parrilla Mexican restaurant in Acworth. While waiting for their order to arrive, the family worked on coming up with a name for a structure resembling an old country porch that had recently been built in the Carp's backyard. Reid directed everyone to write down their desired name for the structure, telling each family member they could vote on one. The only rule was that no one could vote on their own suggestion. When *The Hive* won the name contest, Reid looked a little puzzled. Something seemed a little off in the voting. After some investigation, he realized Kyra had voted for her own choice. She had broken the one and only rule. She smiled mischievously at her husband, and he just grinned and shook his head. If you ever go visit the Carps, you will see a sign for The Hive still adorning the porch structure.

After the family finished their Mexican meal, followed by frozen yogurt at Menchie's, the happy group split up. Daniel and Sydney got in their car, while Reid, Kyra, Livia, and Ellie drove in their borrowed Toyota Tundra. Nolyn rode with Joe, Karen, and Chelsey. Nolyn had asked to ride home with her grandparents so she could enjoy special time with her Nonna. All three vehicles drove out of the Menchie's parking lot at the same time.

Nolyn got in her pajamas and climbed into Nonna's bed to watch television while waiting for her family to return. After about fifteen minutes, Nolyn went into the living room where Chelsey and Joe were relaxing. With a puzzled look on her face, she asked, "When will Mommy get home?"

Joe looked at his phone and realized that Reid and Kyra should have already arrived. Chelsey texted Kyra. No response. Joe and Karen both started calling Reid and Kyra's phones. Still no answer.

Karen told her six-year-old granddaughter, "Maybe they stopped by the store. Don't worry, honey, they will be back soon."

Joe and Chelsey tried to think of reasons why neither Reid nor Kyra would pick up their phones. Finally Chelsey suggested they backtrack to Menchie's to see if they could find them. Karen stayed with Nolyn.

Joe and Chelsey carefully retraced the same roads they had driven home having no idea that Reid had taken a different route. Joe called Reid's brother-in-law, Kyle Vance, to see if perhaps Reid and Kyra had stopped by there for a last-minute visit. When Kyle said he hadn't seen them, Joe really began to worry. Chelsey and Joe took turns calming each other down as they tried to figure out what was happening. Menchie's was closing when they got there, but one worker was standing at the door. Chelsey ran up to ask they had seen her sister and family. Maybe they had returned to Menchie's because they left something. Joe's anxiety grew when the worker said, "No, I am so sorry. They didn't come back here." Joe decided to go back to Cartersville via Highway 41, also known as GA Highway 3.

Joe first called Cobb County and then Bartow County Police Departments to see if any accidents had been reported. There were no reports. This information gave Joe a moment of reprieve from worry. Then he decided to call the Emerson Police Station. When Joe gave them his name and asked if there had been any accidents, he was put on hold. This had not happened when he had called the other two stations.

When the operator picked back up, Joe was almost begging her to tell him what she knew. At this point Chelsey said, "Dad, please pull over to the side of the road." As Joe pulled over, the police operator came back on the line to tell him someone would be in contact soon. This infuriated Joe.

While he was on the phone with Emerson PD, Karen beeped in. "Joe, I need you to come home right now." Joe was visibly shaken as he asked her to please tell him what was happening. Karen just kept asking him to come home.

As they tried to make their way home, they soon saw numerous flashing lights in the distance. They could not see the actual accident because of backed up traffic and the many emergency vehicles blocking the view. Joe drove as close as he could to the barricade. He finally was able to talk to two nearby policemen.

"Sirs, my name is Joe Carp, and I am looking for my daughter and son-in-law."

"Mr. Carp, you need to go home. All we can tell you is that two little girls have been rushed to the children's hospital."

Joe, with his heart beating out of his chest, tried to stabilize his weak knees. He now knew that the blinking lights and stopped traffic in front of him were for his family. With a knot in his stomach and tears in his eyes, he called Sydney and asked her and Daniel to come to the house. Joe also called Kyle back and gave him an update.

Karen was glad she had shut her bedroom door where

Nolyn was sound asleep in her bed.

When Joe arrived back home, he froze when he saw the police car in his yard. He fell into his wife's arms as she said, "There has been an accident. Kyra didn't make it."

Karen went into protective mode. In her mind she could hear Kyra saying, *Mom, get it together. My babies need you right now.*

In Five Seconds

As Reid drove along Highway 41 N., Kyra reminisced about the fun evening with her family and looked forward to morning coffee with her three high-school friends. As they approached the Zep plant on the hill above the highway, a driverless semi delivery truck careened down the driveway and smashed into the passenger side of the vehicle. Shoved violently across the median, the crushed vehicle only stopped when it hit the guard rail of the opposite lane. Emergency vehicles arrived within minutes. The first responders labored for nearly two hours to get everyone out of the twisted vehicle.

The Tundra they were driving was bent in the middle, so Reid could not see Kyra or his girls in the back. He could hear Ellie and Livia whimpering behind him, but the silence from Kyra's side was deafening. He was trapped and could not move to answer the ringing cell phones. All he could do was call out to God and try to calm the girls with words of comfort.

After Reid was freed from the vehicle and was finally able to talk to an emergency worker, he asked, "Did my wife make it?"

"Sir, we believe she died instantly."

In five seconds, Kyra's dash ended. In five seconds, everything changed.

At the Hospitals

Karen, Chelsey, and Sydney drove to Scottish Rite Children's Hospital where four-year-old Ellie and two-year-old Livia had been transported by two separate ambulances.

Joe, Daniel, and Nolyn drove to Kennestone Hospital where the third ambulance had taken Reid. They had awakened Nolyn and told her they were going to see her family.

Kyle and Alexis drove to tell Reid's mom, Janet, about the accident and then drove her to see Reid. They met Reid's brother Jared at the hospital.

Karen drove Chelsey and Sydney to Scottish Rite. Her heart broke as she listened to the painful cries of her other two daughters. She knew she needed prayer support, so she called her good friend Melody Pendley.

It was after 11:00 p.m. when Melody's phone rang. "Hello."

Karen replied, "Melody, Kyra was killed in an accident. Please pray for us."

"What? What are you saying?" Melody sat up in her bed as she listened to Karen repeat the dreadful words.

"Where are you?" Melody stood up to walk into the den where her husband, Lamar, was watching television.

"I am on my way to Scottish Rite Hospital to see the girls. Joe has gone to Kennestone Hospital to check on Reid."

Melody and Lamar quickly headed to Kennestone to be with Reid and Joe. On the way she called more good friends, including Tim and Cathy Smith and Steve and Tonia McCombs.

The Smiths met the Pendleys at Kennestone. Lamar and Tim stayed with Joe as he waited with Reid, while Cathy and Melody drove to Scottish Rite. On the way to the children's hospital, they stopped by Walmart and purchased two new car seats.

When Reid first saw Joe, Kyle, and Jared, in his shock he kept repeating the sentence, "Kyra is gone. She is with the Lord." Through his tears, he praised the Lord because he knew where his wife was. His faith had taken a hard hit, but he held on to it as hard as he could.

The emergency doctors suggested keeping Reid for observation, but he wanted to get to his children. He was the one who told Nolyn about her mommy, and she stayed as close as possible by his side. He was released after a few hours, and Joe drove him and Nolyn to Scottish Rite. Reid broke down at the sight of his two youngest daughters. It was around 2:00 a.m. when Livia was released from hospital care. Reid stayed with Ellie, who was released later in the day. Her casted right leg was propped up in her small wheelchair as the nurse rolled her out of the hospital.

A Life of Simple Surrender

On August 19, 2015, friends and family gathered at Tabernacle Baptist Church to celebrate Kyra's life. Lindy Cooper once again sang "Turn Your Eyes Upon Jesus" as guests were welcomed into a time of worship. We then listened to words that reflected Kyra's life journey.

Every day we are living out words that will one day be voiced about our life. We will not hear those words, but the people we leave behind will hang on to every spoken sentence.

Kyra often prayed the words of the psalmist in Psalm 19:14: "May these words of my mouth and this meditation of my heart be pleasing in your sight, Lord, my Rock and my Redeemer." She wanted her words to point everyone around her to the love of Jesus. Even more, she wanted to mirror the grace that had been extended to her.

Kyra did not complicate her relationship with Jesus. She just walked with Him in simple surrender.

19

The Goodness of the Lord: 15 Devotions from Kyra's Prayer Journal and Stories

Proclaiming the Goodness of the Lord

> *My mouth will tell of your righteous deeds, of
> your saving acts all day long—though I know
> not how to relate them all. I will come and
> proclaim your mighty acts, Sovereign LORD; I
> will proclaim your righteous deeds, yours alone.
> Since my youth, God, you have taught me, and
> to this day I declare your marvelous deeds.*
> Psalm 71:15–17

The circle of Kyra's life is complete. Her spirit lives in heaven where there is no more sorrow and no more pain. With this knowledge, why would her prayers written years ago matter to anybody? Why would she care about or even want her beliefs shared with people still in this world?

Kyra lived a life of freedom. What does a life of freedom look like? If you watched Kyra, it looked like a lot of laughter and a lot of love. She woke up in the morning knowing that her day would hold more than what the natural eye could see. She pursued a heart that would love God and others. In that pursuit, she was able to do life without a lot of worldly baggage. Her obedience to God's Word freed her from the tyranny of materialism and expectations that challenge us all. Her freedom came not from being a perfect person but from seeking the perfect person of Jesus Christ.

Kyra wanted others to experience the joy she found in following Jesus. She asked God to help her not be silent about His saving acts. The compilation of prayers in Kyra's journal and stories of her well-lived life speak loudly of the faithfulness of God. Even during her times of heartache and pain, she spoke of the goodness of the Lord.

> *Lord, I see again and again the importance of telling others what you are doing in my life. May I not keep silent but obey the Holy Spirit.*
> ~ Kyra's Journal

She may not be physically present to share the goodness of the Lord with you, but through her written prayers and stories, may you sense your own invitation to spiritual freedom.

A Fun Friend Comfortable in Her Own Skin

*For you created my inmost being; you knit
me together in my mother's womb. I praise
you because I am fearfully and wonderfully
made; your works are wonderful, I know that
full well. My frame was not hidden from you
when I was made in the secret place, when
I was woven together in the depths of the
earth. Your eyes saw my unformed body; all
the days ordained for me were written in your
book before one of them came to be.*
Psalm 139:13–16

I want to represent Kyra well. She would not want anyone to think she had it all together or that she was perfect in any way. She struggled with life and its complexities just like you and me. Yet there is one thing that stood out about her: she knew her Creator and she trusted Him. This was her baseline in how she responded to life. It gave her the ability to love God, others, and herself.

Kyra had a knack for making friends. I think it was because she knew how to be a friend to herself. She was confident that since God valued her, He also valued others. She made it her goal early in life to be herself and simply love others the way God loved her.

Kyra's friend Dan Pohl said it best.

> In middle school and high school, everybody was very concerned with being "cool," myself included. I should say almost everybody, because Kyra never cared about what people categorized her as. She was always herself: extremely kind, generous, inclusive, and lots of fun. While everybody was trying their hardest to be cool, Kyra just was.

She was one grade ahead of me, so she got her license before I did. Since we lived in the same neighborhood, we decided that she would pick me up every morning and take me to school with her. (I only had my learner's permit, but sometimes I would drive so she could get ready in the mirror. Oops.) Before long, she invited me to her house in the mornings to drink coffee before we left for school. I absolutely agreed because Kyra was somebody you simply wanted to be around whenever you had the chance. We did this routine for a little while, and though I usually hated waking up earlier than I had to, this was something I wasn't going to miss. What I never told Kyra, though, was that I hated coffee. I never drank it before and didn't enjoy it then, but had I mentioned that, I may have lost those mornings with one of the most genuine, compassionate, encouraging, and coolest people that I knew.

I cannot imagine how many people have felt special like I did when they were around Kyra. I know that her life's impact will last for generations and Jesus will be spoken about and believed in because of her. Thank you, God, for a friend like that.

Because of Kyra's authentic relationship with God, she was able to live in freedom—freedom to love and accept herself and freedom to love and accept others.

Am I now trying to win the approval of human beings or of God? Or am I trying to please people? If I were still trying to please people, I would not be a servant of Christ. (Galatians 1:10)

Comparison is the death of contentment!
~ Kyra's Journal

What would it look like for you to live each day with the knowledge that you are fully loved and accepted by God?

How much energy do you use comparing yourself to others?

Tension Within

*I do not understand what I do. For what I want
to do I do not do, but what I hate I do.... For
in my inner being I delight in God's law; but
I see another law at work in me, waging war
against the law of my mind and making me a
prisoner of the law of sin at work within me.*
Romans 7:15, 22–23

Sharon Mauldin, Kyra's Sunday school leader, knew
that Kyra had gotten a small tattoo on her left wrist. She
also knew that Kyra had not told her parents about the
tattoo. The tattoo was not the issue for Miss Sharon. What
brought tension was the fact that Kyra had hidden her tattoo from her parents. Her trendy bracelets covered up the
small marking and kept it hidden from view.

For her tattoo, Kyra had chosen a little star, representing a
shining light, and the numbers 19 and 119. The 19 represented
the location of the book of Psalms, the nineteenth book in the
Bible, and 119 stood for the longest chapter in Psalms. Each of
the 176 verses in Psalm 119 reflect on God's Word.

Kyra had a deep love for the Bible. She genuinely
believed and lived by the words, "Your word is a lamp for
my feet, a light onto my path" (Psalm 119:105). The tattoo represented her beliefs, yet it brought her unrest in her
spirit. At eighteen she was free to make the decision. Still,
she experienced a pull between what she had done and not
wanting to disappoint her parents. Even the knowledge of
their unconditional love did not bring her to a comfort level
of full disclosure.

Several Sundays passed, and Kyra was still covering up
the tattoo with bracelets. Sharon could see the conflict in
Kyra's eyes. Not only did she discern Kyra's lack of peace,

but she also felt her own stress about the situation. After praying for wisdom to know how to balance accountability with her love for Kyra, Sharon approached the teen. "Kyra, I see you are struggling with telling your parents about the tattoo. I would really encourage you to tell your mom."

Kyra calmly replied with tears in her eyes, "Thank you, Miss Sharon. This has been lying heavy on my heart, and I know that I must tell my parents today." That is exactly what she did.

Once Kyra was able to surrender her inner battle and experience true vulnerability with her parents, her peace returned. She removed the bracelets, and the light in her eyes returned.

It is a good sign if you are experiencing spiritual tension, as Kyra did. Embrace the struggle and fight for the win.

Kyra wrote the following words in her journal almost eight years after her tattoo story:

> I needed a slap in the face to realize that I cannot continue in my sin. Just like the verse I have taped to my closet: "Do not be deceived: God cannot be mocked. A man reaps what he sows." I have reaped what I have sown. It is so easy for me to recognize my sin but then quickly point out all the ways I have been wronged. O God, forgive me. I know this is wrong. Change my heart. Teach me how to be quick to confess and repent no matter what. I cannot do it without you.

Even though Kyra was married, a mother, and a missionary, she still at times battled the tension in her soul— the war of the flesh. She was thankful for people who cared enough about her to call her out when she wasn't headed in the right direction.

Through her ability to welcome accountability with honesty and authenticity, Kyra had the freedom to feel the tension and ask God and others for help in her struggles.

Where is your spiritual tension today?

Are you open to listening to God through another person?

Who in your circle of connections can offer you accountability?

Feet that Carry Encouragement

*And how can anyone preach unless they are
sent? As it is written, "How beautiful are the
feet of those who bring good news!"*
Romans 10:15

Kyra loved shoes. Shopping for shoes was one of her favorite pastimes, and she also cherished any opportunity to help other people pick out their shoes. Her favorite stores were thrift shops, but she would bargain hunt at any shopping complex. Her appreciation for shoes made her aware of all the different shoes that would pass her every day.

Imagine sitting on a busy sidewalk eye level with all the legs, strollers, walkers, crutches, or wheelchairs that are passing in front of you. There are all types and sizes of shoes, each carrying a person who is experiencing any range of emotions, from deep sadness to exhilarating joy. Some shoes may be carrying a person who is slowly putting one step in front of the other, their legs heavy with sorrow. Some shoes are passing by quickly, and some are even skipping to their own inner beat. The shoes may be carrying tired older people or runaway toddlers. Some feet are clad with casts or orthopedic boots where there has been an injury.

Especially in the western world, we love and value shoes, but we do not always value the people inside the shoes.

Kyra noticed not only the shoes of those around her, but she also noticed the people wearing the shoes. She had a way of stepping into someone else's shoes to view the world from their perspective. Even as a young person, Kyra was dependent on God to help her have patience with those around her. No matter what her family or friends were walking through, she tried to exude patience and understanding.

Years ago on a Sunday at church, seventeen-year-old

Kyra walked up and asked me where I got my shoes. A sense of confidence entered my soul after hearing a teenager compliment my choice of fashion. Kyra explained that she was hoping to find some shoes like mine for her prom. Smiling, I told her I thought I'd bought them at Payless Shoes because they sold shoes that fit my wide foot. Kyra laughed and again complimented my taste. She had noticed my shoes, which prompted her to encourage me.

The Bible verse at the beginning of this devotional mentions the beauty of feet that carry the gospel of Christ. Indeed, how beautiful are the feet of those who steer others to a life of victory and freedom found through trusting and following Jesus Christ.

One characteristic of being an encourager is patience. Patience with whomever is hurting or lost in a spiral of confusion. Patience to share the good news without pushing it down someone's throat. Patience to not judge based on appearance.

Courage is another characteristic of encouragers. One must be ready for rejection or being misunderstood when offering encouragement, especially in a world that so often rejects the message of the gospel.

Kyra exemplified patience as she walked into the dark streets of Rome to try to befriend women who had landed in the invisible cage of sex trafficking. She trained with the Green Light Project to safely know how to talk with the girls. She wanted them to know that if they wanted to rid their shoes of sex slavery, she and her team would do whatever they could to provide new shoes along with a new life.

Even though Kyra had only been involved with the Green Light Project for a short time before her death, she intentionally walked with courage and patience into a world of darkness. She walked there because of her deep love for people.

Love is patient. We bend over in humility to help a scraped person because we know it takes a lifetime to learn how to walk with Jesus. Love always begins with patience. Patience is a willingness to suffer.

~ Kyra's Journal

Who can you take a moment to encourage today?

In which of your relationships is God calling you to walk in patience and courage?

Aunt Kicky's Happies

Remembering the words the Lord Jesus himself
said, "It is more blessed to give than to receive."
Acts 20:35

From the moment Kyra was born, Vicki Howard, the only sister of Karen Howard Carp, fell in love with her first niece. Since Kyra could not say "Vicki," she renamed her "Aunt Kicky." As a toddler, Kyra quickly understood that when Aunt Kicky came around, there would be a little gift behind her back. All the love gifts became known as *happies*. As Kyra and her sisters grew older, the happies became more expensive.

My favorite happy story occurred when Kyra was in college.

"Heather, there are a lot of shoe sales going on in downtown Athens," Kyra informed her friend as she walked into her dorm room. Kyra knew that Heather loved shoes as much as she did.

"Kyra, I don't have any money to buy shoes right now," Heather replied.

Kyra coaxed, "Oh, come on, Heather. Take a break from all this studying and come dream with me about shoes that we might one day be able to purchase. We can just window shop."

Remembering that her friend was always the mastermind of fun experiences, Heather put her books aside and jumped in the car with Kyra.

The shoe stores were crowded, but it did not take long for the girls to find the best sale at a hole-in-the-wall store. The perfect boots jumped out at Heather and Kyra.

Sadly, Heather moaned, "I knew this might happen. When I have money, I cannot find what I want. Now that I found what I want, I don't have any money."

Kyra stopped in her tracks, looked wide-eyed at Heather, and pulled out her cell phone.

Heather had an idea who Kyra was dialing, so she got up close to hear the conversation.

"Aunt Kicky, hi, it's me. I was just wondering what you think about me getting an early birthday present. Heather and I found some boots, and they are absolutely perfect."

Aunt Kicky was always happy to hear from Kyra. Now was a good time to focus on Kyra as she had just said good-bye to her last second grader for the day. She sat down at her teacher's desk and responded, "Yes, I will be happy to get you some birthday boots. Do you still have my credit card number?"

Kyra said, "Yes. Thank you so much! I just wanted to check with you first. Also, Heather wants to talk with you."

Sensing Kyra's smile through the phone, Aunt Kicky responded, "Sure."

"Aunt Kicky, I was thinking about an Aunt Kicky *happy loan*. I have a new job but have not gotten paid yet. I am not sure if I will ever find any other boots to fit me like these. Would you mind if we also put my boots on your credit card? I promise I will pay you back." Heather tried to not sound too desperate as she came up for breath, yet she really wanted the boots.

Not long after, Heather and Kyra walked out of the store with smiles on their faces and new boots on their feet.

Aunt Kicky, though she lived in another state, was intentional in giving gifts of encouragement to her nieces and their friends. It was more than a material gift; it was the gift of trust with an important financial number.

The joy and blessing that Kyra received from her Aunt Kicky prompted her desire to bestow *happy gifts* of encouragement to her family and friends. Kyra was constantly thinking of ways to encourage people through offerings of personal cards, baked goods, and written prayers. Many times in Italy, she would share pretty containers of her homemade cookies and muffins with families in her neighborhood. She also used words of encouragement to uplift women who looked weary and tired.

It requires vulnerability to offer another person something from your heart. It also requires trusting God for the outcomes when you say yes to actions of love.

> *Jesus, help me not to be so distracted with my life that I neglect the daily opportunities to share your love with those who you strategically place in my path.*
>
> ~ Kyra's Journal

What are some tangible ways for you to share encouragement with those in your sphere of influence?

Who or what can you say yes to even if it might be a risk?

Peace in the Chaos

*Truly my soul finds rest in God, my salvation
comes from him. Truly he is my rock and my salvation, he is my fortress, I will never be shaken.*
Psalm 62:1–2

Kyra was fun and at times mischievous, yet she was cautious and deep in her thinking. She sought to be strongly connected to God, which in turn connected her to people. She desired to authentically represent the peace of God to those around her.

One story stands out when Kyra stayed true to her desire to represent God. She was at a Tabernacle Baptist youth missions adventure in Lac de Flambeau, Wisconsin, in the summer of 2004. Kyra had completed her first year of college and had joined youth pastor Steve McCombs's summer leadership team.

Brother Steve divided the youth and leadership into ministry groups. Kyra was put in charge of one of the groups. She knew that when working with high-school students, she'd have to be ready for anything. One of Kyra's students, Therron Smith, had a run-in with a saw that ripped into his hand. Blood splattered all over Therron as well as the other students standing close by. The alarmed students scattered trying to find help. In her calm way, Kyra took charge. After she wrapped Theron's hand with a clean cloth, she quickly secured him a ride to the nearest hospital, and she notified Therron's mother, Cathy Smith, who was serving with another group on the other side of town.

Cathy rushed to the hospital, ran inside the emergency room door, and rounded the corner just in time to see Kyra's comforting smile. Kyra said, "He is okay, Ms. Cathy." The color returned to Cathy's face as she hugged Kyra.

Later, Cathy reminisced, "When I arrived at the hospital,

Kyra had taken care of everything. All I had to do was go see Therron. She peacefully ministered to me and my son."

Kyra exemplified peace as a college student, then as a married woman, and then as a mother of three active daughters. No matter what was going on around her, she remained calm, did what she could, and then trusted God to do what only He could do. Kyra's journal provides insight to her ability to remain calm in difficult situations.

> I should find rest in God no matter the circumstances. "Don't be afraid, just believe." (Mark 5:36)
>
> Decide to obey and live in freedom, peace, and eternal joy, or decide to ignore His most frequently stated command—do not fear—and live in a constant state of stress.
>
> ~ Kyra's Journal

How are you handling the chaos in your life?

Who is watching you handle your chaos?

Living Authentically

> *"I have the right to do anything," you*
> *say—but not everything is beneficial. "I*
> *have the right to do anything"—but I will*
> *not be mastered by anything. The body is*
> *not meant for sexual immorality but for the*
> *Lord, and the Lord for the body."*
> 1 Corinthians 6:12–13b (Found in Kyra's Journal)

Reid, Kyra, Katie, and Katie's boyfriend, Matt, were looking forward to their upcoming camping trip to the Georgia mountains. The fall air was crisp, the colorful leaves were beautiful, and the wind seemed like it was calling their names.

There was just one little catch. Kyra felt tension in her stomach as she thought about her upcoming conversation with Katie. She practiced in her mind what she would say. She prayed for the right words. Her desire was not to hurt Katie, and she certainly did not want to put a wedge in their friendship. She knew what had to be said, but it was not going to be easy.

"Katie, do you mind if I sleep in your tent? Reid and I have made the decision to not sleep alone in the same room before marriage."

There was a moment of silence as the two friends looked into each other's eyes.

A little surprised, Katie could only think of a question: "Kyra, what is your definition of a room? I mean technically, we will be outside, and you two will not actually be alone."

In recounting this memory, Katie admitted that she could not hide her disappointment over not being able to sleep beside her love. While their friendship was strong enough for

Katie to voice that she felt her friend's conviction was a little silly, she realized that she could not change Kyra's mind. She also knew that her friend was not judging her for her different views. Katie felt heard and accepted by Kyra, and deep down she admired Kyra for sticking to her convictions.

After a weekend of watching Kyra and Reid, Katie realized that they were building a relationship on something much stronger than their physical attraction. Later, Katie and Matt decided to make the same rule for their relationship. Somehow that decision brought out the best in them. They eventually married.

Kyra, in her surrender to God, wanted what He wanted more than what she desired. She and Reid felt freedom to commit to taking purity into their marriage. Kyra also walked in freedom as she was able to be honest with Katie in her actions and in her words.

Where do you struggle living up to your convictions?

Is there a place in your life absent of peace because of your lack of authenticity?

The Song of a Focused Soul

Truly my soul finds rest in God; my salva-
tion comes from Him. Truly, He is my rock
and my salvation, I will never be shaken.
Psalm 62:1–2

The December night was clear with a half-moon shining above the wedding garden. The air was crisp but not cold as the candles flickered around the faces of Kyra, Reid, and the wedding party. The moment was lovely and serene, as a beautiful voice began to sing over the sound system.

> Turn your eyes upon Jesus.
> Look full in His wonderful face.
> And the things of earth will grow strangely dim,
> In the light of His glory and grace.

The song was not a traditional wedding song, but indeed it was a love song. It became clear that Kyra wanted her wedding, and more importantly her marriage, to reflect her first love . . . Jesus.

The title of this powerful hymn is "Turn Your Eyes Upon Jesus," originally titled "The Heavenly Vision." The song was also important to Reid, as it was his dad's favorite hymn.

Kyra enjoyed literary history, so investigating the history behind one of her favorite hymns seems appropriate.

The first historical figure is Lilia (Lily) Trotter. She was born in 1853 in England. Miss Trotter was gifted with an amazing ability to paint watercolor pictures. She was well on her way to becoming a world-renowned artist when she was influenced to go tell the world about Jesus. Dwight L. Moody impacted her life purpose so profoundly that she laid down her paint brush and became a missionary in Algiers, Algeria. Lilia knew how important it was to remain focused on Jesus in a world full of choices. In 1917, she wrote a booklet titled *Focus*. The booklet reflected the beauty of looking to God alone for the needs only He can meet.

Helen Lemmel enters the story at this point. Helen was born in 1863, daughter to a Methodist preacher in England. When she was twelve, she and her family moved to Wisconsin, where she soon became well known for her singing ability. Helen became famous in the secular world and then decided to focus on singing songs that would spiritually encourage the human soul. It was around this turning point in her life that she was given a booklet entitled *Focus*. After reading Lilia's words, Helen was moved to write the hymn, "Turn Your Eyes Upon Jesus." Out of the more than five hundred hymns she wrote, this one is her most famous. It is also the song that kept her strong during the challenges of losing her eyesight, being abandoned, penniless, and alone. When asked how she was doing, Helen would always answer, "I am doing fine in what matters." Indeed, no matter what she had or did not possess, she was fine with only Jesus.

Although Lilia and Helen lived and died many years before Kyra was born, their words impacted the way she lived. In the same way, the impact of Kyra's ministry legacy continues today.

Even when the issues of life clouded Kyra's focus, she always came back to her foundational relationship—Jesus.

> *Lord, in the times my soul is longing after You, help me to recognize what is happening and seek Your face and not try to fill that longing with anything else.*
>
> ~ Kyra's Journal

Who or what do you focus on expecting to find peace, acceptance, and freedom?

Time with Jesus: A Sister's Perspective

Seek the LORD and his strength.
Seek his face always.
1 Chronicles 16:11

Rome was hustling with holiday activity. The streets were crowded, the Christmas music was loud, and the aroma of Italian cooking filled the air. The festive atmosphere added to the joy of being with Kyra. Chelsey had visited Kyra in Rome before, but being with her during the biggest birthday celebration of the year was exceptional.

Kyra cooked with fresh ingredients, which meant daily errands to the Italian supermarket or the streetside fresh food stands. She always invited Chelsey to walk with her for her daily errands so they could also explore new spots along the way. Chelsey did not want to miss any adventure that might happen by just being in Kyra's presence. She felt the anticipation of what lay ahead. Who would Kyra smile at, which in turn would spark a conversation in Italian? What obscure, hole-in-the-wall place would they visit just for fun? What would they find if they went to the Repeat Store where Kyra loved to bargain hunt? It was always so much fun to search through the hundreds of donated items for sale. On a chilly, December day, as the two sisters wandered to the Repeat Store, neither one suspected that this would be Kyra's last Christmas season on earth.

Kyra picked out something for her kitchen, a button-down shirt for Reid, and a cute blouse for herself. Chelsey noticed Kyra's furrowed brow and pursed lips staring intently at the blouse. After a few moments, Kyra looked at her sister and decided, "This blouse is cute, but I don't need it."

Chelsey responded, "Kyra! It is only three euros. Even if you don't need it, three euros is not that much. Just let me purchase it for you."

Kyra had made up her mind that the three euros could be better spent on another shirt for Reid, who did need some more clothes for work. "I don't need it, Chelsey."

As she listened to her sister's explanation, Chelsey realized that this adventure lay in the gift of seeing her sister's sincere heart. Kyra was genuine in her pursuit of Jesus Christ, and the little decisions she made along the way reflected that passion. Kyra found freedom in saying yes to a shirt for her husband. She paid attention to the tension of the best way to steward her money. It seemed so effortless for Kyra to make a selfless decision, but Chelsey knew that Kyra had spent much time with God asking Him for a heart that was like His.

> Since Kyra made an effort to make Jesus very important in her life, the characteristics of Jesus came out of her more effortlessly. The more time she spent with Jesus, the more she became like Him. After all, we reflect who we surround ourselves with.
>
> ~ Chelsey Carp

SPENDING TIME WITH GOD IS THE MOST IMPORTANT THING.
~ Kyra's Journal (caps are hers)

Just like in any healthy relationship, when you love someone, you want to spend time with them. When was the last time you spent time with God?

What fear or disappointment is keeping you from sitting still before the Lord?

Taking Time to Remember

*I will remember the deeds of the Lord; yes,
I will remember your miracles of long ago. I
will consider all your works and meditate on
all your mighty deeds.*
Psalm 77:11–12

Kyra's high-school youth group at Tabernacle Baptist Church encouraged students to live for Jesus at home and abroad. Their camaraderie with each other strengthened their individual journeys with God. Several of the youth from that time stepped out in faith to live out the gospel in other parts of the world.

Kyra's death was painful and left a hole in the close group. They had to choose to remember the cherished times with Kyra and trust God with His plan.

Stephen Corey was in the youth group the same time as Kyra. He has fond memories of going over to Kyra's and playing basketball with her dad, whom he called Mr. Joe. Later, as a fellow missionary, he developed a friendship with Kyra and Reid.

> My fondest memory of Kyra is when we both were starting a new adventure. We were both about to be missionaries overseas. I remember her and Reid inviting me to ride with them to our training in Virginia in a hand-me-down Honda Accord that somebody had given them. We packed that thing full! It was Kyra and Reid in the front, baby Nolyn and me in the back, with a bunch of suitcases piled up in the back seat, trunk, and on top of the car. I remember the excitement that we all were sharing in starting a new life, leaving everything behind. Our eyes gleamed with anticipation as we drove to our FPO (Field Personnel Orien-

tation). It was all we could think about and talk about. We were nervous, anxious, excited, and ready to be overseas. When we finally got there, we met more than three hundred people that were also exiting their comfort zones.

During our time at orientation, we would regularly eat meals together. When I was finished eating, I carried Nolyn around the cafeteria. I quickly became known as Uncle Coco.

I remember that Kyra had already learned some Italian. During a worship service we had one day, in front of our peers, she stood and read from the Bible in Italian. It flowed out of her mouth perfectly. It was then that I thought God has been preparing Kyra. I mean look, she already speaks the language! He had been preparing her throughout her life for this type of work. All the other missionaries were amazed at how she was already equipped to begin the work. The rest of us were just getting ready to start language training.

I had a special bond with Kyra and Reid. Anyone who serves overseas long-term understands the challenges and can gain comfort from each other.

When I got the news that Kyra had died, I think it was the first time that I had ever really mourned in my life. It was a very hard time. I will always remember how God used Kyra to point me to a true, surrendered relationship with Jesus. I rejoice that I will one day see her in eternity.

~ Stephen Corey

We will all face times of heartache and trials. If we will take time to recall people and circumstances who God has used in our lives, His goodness will come to light and His hope will once again fill our souls.

Kyra did not give any specifics surrounding the following prayer. She simply remembered God's faithfulness during her struggles.

Wow, this has been the hardest time of my life. As I sit here thinking and trying to figure out how to pray, I am thankful to God my Rock and my Redeemer. "Yet this I call to mind and therefore I have hope: because of the Lord's great love we are not consumed, for his compassions never fail. They are new every morning, great is your faithfulness." (Lamentations 3:21–23)

~ Kyra's Journal

Everyone has experienced some type of loss. In our dislike of pain, we often do not take time to grieve those losses. What or whom have you lost recently?

Have you taken time to grieve?

Poor in Spirit

Blessed are the poor in spirit,
for theirs is the kingdom of heaven.
Matthew 5:3

Kyra listened intently to Pastor Leo and his wife Valeria. She felt overwhelmed as they explained the challenges of church planting in Rome. She knew it was beyond her ability to live and serve among the Italian people. She was far from the comforts of her American home, far from feeling adequate to be a missionary of the gospel. She knew she was "poor in spirit."

Jesus challenged his listeners to recognize their spiritual poverty and to recognize a need for God. He said that we are blessed if we know we are poor spiritually. The moment we realize that we have a need for spiritual guidance, we have been blessed . . . we have been handed something good.

Kyra recognized her spiritual need at a young age. She decided early that her spiritual decisions influenced every other area of her life. She embraced Psalm 119:105: "Your word is a lamp for my feet, a light on my path." Truly, in a dark world, she recognized that she needed a bright Light to help her see where she was going. Being poor in spirit helped her to be aware of her need for God's guidance and intervention.

On that day in Pastor Leo and Valeria's living room in Rome, Reid sat beside Kyra on the couch. Baby Nolyn wiggled on Kyra's lap. It was a hot day without air conditioning, so the windows were open. With her firstborn on her lap and her husband sitting beside her, she looked into Pastor Leo's eyes and said, "We know it will be hard. It will take a long time to build relationships of trust when it comes to church planting, but we are in this for a lifetime. We cannot do this, but God can."

Kyra lived a life in which she desired God above all else.

I can better understand what Jesus meant when he said, "Blessed are the poor in spirit" (Matthew 5:3). Indeed, Kyra was blessed. As she lived her life in need of God, she was able to unselfishly love her husband, children, family, friends, and the Italian people who became her family. Now she is blessed most of all as she abides in the presence of the One she loved the most.

> *Lord, I need your help. I am prideful and selfish, and I need you to change me. I want to be like you. I don't even know what to pray for, but your Spirit intercedes with groans for me. O Lord, I want to hunger for your word. I don't want to fill myself with what does not satisfy.*
>
> ~ Kyra's Journal

What is the situation in your life where you feel weak or inadequate?

What would it take for you to surrender that situation to God?

"I Felt Valued by Her"

A new command I give you: Love one another.
As I have loved you, so you must love one
another. By this everyone will know that you
are my disciples, if you love one another.
John 13:34–35

The Karrs became friends with Amy and Josh Carpenter and their three children during one stateside visit. The Carpenters were members of Tabernacle Baptist, the Karrs' sending church. The year after Kyra's death, the Carpenters moved to Rome to work beside Reid and the other missionaries.

Amy shared these thoughts about Kyra:

> I will never forget riding in the back of a pickup truck on the Fourth of July with Kyra. She was throwing water balloons at our husbands and kids, who were taking a leisurely stroll near us. The laughter of that memory still brings joy to my heart. I admired that Kyra loved deeply but did not take herself or others too seriously. When I think of Kyra, I think LOVE. In her absence I find great inspiration to love beyond my wildest imagination. I find courage and boldness to try things we many not otherwise try, because I realize life on earth is short. I find freedom to let go of all that hinders and snares me, and I run toward the prize with perseverance and endurance. The little things that once mattered do not matter anymore because love covers a multitude of things.
>
> I discover that long after I leave this world my life will continue to have an impact. The choices I make every day really do matter. For example, what I say or don't say, how I treat others and make others feel. If I focus on love, it will affect how I spend my time.
>
> Kyra inspired me to stop and ask myself if what

I am doing really matters and how will it affect those I love once I am gone. My relationship with Kyra taught me that above all things, love is the greatest. She loved so big! Her hugs were some of my favorites because she would squeeze me tight every time she saw me. I felt valued by her.

Today Josh and Amy continue to help to build loving, grace-filled communities in Italy.

> *Lord, by your spirit help me hate what is evil and cling to what is good. Romans 12:10: "Be devoted to one another in brotherly love. Honor one another above yourselves." I can only do this by your grace, O Lord.*
>
> ~ Kyra's Journal

Who in your life inspires you to put others before yourself?

Who do you inspire to do the same?

The Pause in the Park

*Let your conversation be always full of
grace, seasoned with salt, so that you may
know how to answer everyone.*
Colossians 4:6

Kyra and Laura had fun expectations for their last walk before Kyra and her family had to return to Rome. Their two-month stateside visit had gone by way too fast.

It was a hot August morning as Laura watched her best friend drive into Sam Smith Park. She could see Kyra smiling and waving at her through the windshield. After Kyra parked, her three little ones piled out of the car. Each little blonde head popped out with a smile for Laura.

Laura grinned as she observed Kyra unloading bikes for Nolyn and Ellie, who were six and four at the time, and the stroller for two-year-old Livia.

The friends walked side by side as they pushed the strollers holding Laura's daughter, Ebby, and Livia. The moms kept their eyes on Nolyn and Ellie as the girls rode their bikes several yards ahead. The two friends chatted and laughed at how their lives had changed from the days when they walked in the park as teenagers.

The adult conversation came to a halt after about ten minutes when things began to unravel. Ellie whined that she was tired and told Kyra that she was not going to make it for the rest of the outing. It was in that moment that Livia had to go potty. In the middle of Ellie's emotional breakdown, Kyra took Livia to potty in the woods that bordered the walking track.

Laura thought, *I already feel exhausted, and we just got started.* Their fun had quickly turned into a chaotic experience.

With Livia more comfortable, Kyra turned to a completely dismantled Ellie. In a moment when a mother would normally throw up her hands, admit defeat, pack up the kids, and head home, Kyra simply walked over to her middle daughter, knelt beside her, and asked, "Ellie, what is going on?"

Ellie answered through her tears, "My legs hurt, and I can't do it."

"Do you want me to pray with you?"

Ellie nodded yes, and Kyra prayed over her daughter, asking the Lord to strengthen her legs and help her to continue.

Observing the intimate moments between a mother and her daughter, Laura's thoughts turned from thinking the outing was a complete disaster to amazement at Kyra's grace and patience. The walk on the trail continued as the laughter of little girls once again began to fill the air.

There are many times in our lives when we look forward to something, but after a good beginning, things go south. Kyra had learned the art of taking a pause in a difficult circumstance. In that pause, she simply asked for God to give her his wisdom and grace and then extended it to her daughter. This was one example of how Kyra took her faith into every interaction with family, friends, and even strangers.

> *Thank you, God, for meeting all my needs*
> *and desires. I am so undeserving of your love*
> *and mercy, and yet you give it so freely. May*
> *I in turn do the same to all around me.*
>
> ~ Kyra's Journal

Who or what situation in your life is begging for a pause?

How can you extend grace to those you love the most?

Sister Love

Love is patient, love is kind. It does not envy,
it does not boast, it is not proud. It does not
dishonor others, it is not self-seeking, it is not
easily angered, it keeps no record of wrongs.
Love does not delight in evil but rejoices with
the truth. It always protects, always trusts,
always hopes, always perseveres.
1 Corinthians 13:4–7

In 2002, singer Michelle Branch, who was only a year and a half older than Kyra, scheduled a concert in Centennial Olympic Park. Kyra looked forward to listening to Michelle's songs off her album *The Spirit Room.* "Everywhere," "You Get Me," and "All You Wanted" were on the top of Kyra's list of songs that she couldn't wait to hear Michelle sing. In anticipation of a star-filled summer night of music, Kyra planned to drive down to Atlanta with a few of her friends to hear the young musician.

Then Kyra thought of her sisters. They were both in middle school and might enjoy Michelle's music. Kyra had a moment of internal debate over whether her friends would be okay with middle schoolers joining the group. Then she decided, *My sisters are my friends, and I want them with me at this concert. They will enjoy the experience.*

Kyra's sisters were her first two friends. Although very different in temperaments, Kyra, Chelsey, and Sydney trusted and respected each other, and Kyra took her role as the oldest sister very seriously. The starlit concert was enjoyable for Kyra and her friends, yet it was more than just a concert for Chelsey and Sydney. It was proof that their sister loved them and enjoyed their company.

Chelsey and Sydney have many sister stories that highlight their homegrown love for each other, such as when Kyra convinced Sydney's boyfriend to travel all the way to Rome to propose!

Another surprise also demonstrates the sisters' love, but this time it was for Kyra. In December 2014, Chelsey flew to Rome to visit Kyra and family during the Christmas season. Upon arrival, she presented Kyra with a poem revealing a trip the next day to Marseille, France. Marseille is one of the largest exporters of lavender in the world, and Kyra loved lavender. In joyful camaraderie, Kyra and Chelsey had an amazing time walking the streets amid the intoxicating aroma of the lavender. Missing Sydney, they bought her some lavender-infused goodies. This surprise trip was an amazing gift to Kyra from her sister.

Kyra instilled that same sisterly love in her girls. Late on the night of the accident that took Kyra's life, Chelsey went into the bedroom to check on the girls, who were six and two at the time. (Four-year-old Ellie was still at the hospital.) A distraught and crying Livia was asking for her mommy. When Chelsey stuck her head inside the door, big sister Nolyn, lying beside Livia with her arm around her said, "It is okay, Aunt Chelsey. I have her."

May my interactions with my children be characterized by love.

~ Kyra's Journal

Which of your family relationships could be strengthened by you building a bridge of love?

How are you modeling love for the children in your life?

A Home Built on the Rock

Therefore everyone who hears these words of mine and puts them into practice is like a wise man who built his house on the rock. The rain came down, the streams rose, and the winds blew and beat against that house; yet it did not fall because it had its foundation on the rock.
Matthew 7:24-25

Joe Carp gave a beautiful tribute to Kyra at her celebration of life:

> And finally, as I stand here in this situation today—myself; my wonderful, beautiful wife; my two precious daughters, Chelsey and Sydney; Reid; Reid's mother, Janet; Reid's brother and sisters—we stand here today, and we, without a shadow, of a doubt know that God orchestrated this whole event. If the world were listening, they would say, "You are crazy." He has orchestrated it 100 percent. He has done it for His glory. We do not understand it. That is the Rock we are standing on.

I listened to this daddy as he stood tall in front of more than six hundred people. He represented his family in the midst of an unthinkable tragedy. He took his broken heart and surrendered it to the only One who would never leave him nor forsake him. Joe decided long before Kyra's accident to always put faith before feelings.

What does a home secure on the Rock look like? For Kyra, it began with having a mother who treasured her and a daddy who was devoted to making sure she had what she needed. The good news about Kyra's family is that they embraced their imperfection. If one made a mistake, it was acknowledged. Grace was extended, and life moved forward. Kyra's story is about an imperfect family that decided early on to allow God's grace to rule each relationship.

Karen and Joe are the first ones to admit they did not do everything right in their parenting journey. In fact, like most parents, they have a few regrets. However, there are four values they displayed that gave Kyra her solid foundation: love, honesty, trust, and serving others.

Kyra observed her mom and dad loving each other. She heard her mom and dad talk about the hard things. She saw them embrace after a disagreement. Kyra watched her parents work hard to provide a home infused with unconditional love.

Joe worked at having a home built on the Rock. He deliberately did things for Kyra that demonstrated the value she held in his eyes and in the eyes of God.

Linda Kellogg expressed one example. She worked in the office at Cartersville High School when Kyra, as a senior, was her student assistant:

> When Kyra worked in my office as a student, sometimes her daddy would bring her lunch. He was always so kind and thoughtful toward her. No wonder she knew how to display patience and love toward others.

Thank you, Joe, for standing up in front of your family and friends with an unshakable faith. Your faith in God added to my own journey of searching for true faith amid life's storms.

Lead me to the Rock that is higher than I.
This is my prayer, Lord.
~ Kyra's Journal

Who or what is your life and home built on?

How will your home withstand the inevitable storms of life?

20

Reflections

The words spoken at Kyra's celebration of life provide a glimpse of her legacy.

Reid

I'll be brief this morning, but I wanted to try to find some way to tell you all how thankful we are. We've been humbled and overwhelmed and blown away by the love and the support and the kindness and the prayers for us. Starting with our family, who has just gone above and beyond to be there with us every minute since this happened and to help me with the girls—to help us with the girls and comfort us. To our family here at Tabernacle and our friends here in Cartersville and beyond. And to our church family at Breccia de Roma in Rome and our family there and beyond throughout Italy. To our IMB International Mission Board colleagues, both past and present, who have traveled thousands and thousands of miles to be here and to show their love and support for us. It's just impossible to comprehend, and I'm just trying to find some way to say thank you.

So if you don't already know, I'm sure in this time that we have together you'll see that the most important thing—the single most important thing in Kyra's life—was her relationship with Jesus Christ. That's who she was. It made her who she was. It made her the friend that she was to so many of you—the sister to her sisters, and the daughter to Joe and Karen, and the incredible mom she was to our three little girls, and the wife that she was to me. There are no words to describe how amazing of a wife that she was.

If you see an apple tree, you know it's an apple tree because there are apples hanging on it. It's unmistakable; nobody can tell you otherwise. In the same way, the Bible says on many occasions that a life that's truly been transformed by Christ is unmistakable by the fruit that it produces. I think that what we are seeing here this morning, and what we will see, is that Kyra's life produced a lot of fruit. It's unmistakable that she was a follower of Christ. I think the most amazing indication of that is that despite the horrible and seemingly unjust tragedy that's led to us being here this morning, at the same time the name of Jesus Christ is honored, is glorified, and is definitely praised. There's not a single person on the face of this earth who can explain that. It's unexplainable. It's just simply the fruit of a life transformed by Christ, who lived for Christ, and that's what Kyra was, and that's what she would have. That's what honors her as we are gathered here this morning.

The hope that the believer has, the hope that I have—and it's an amazing hope and promise—is that this is temporary. The Bible is very clear that Kyra is in the presence of Jesus now and that one day all who trust in Christ as their Savior will be there too. There will be no more pain and suffering there. There will be no more tragedies. So I praise the Lord for that and find peace and hope in that. It's an amazing hope and promise for the life transformed by Christ.

But again, just know how thankful I am, and how thankful we are as a family. We are extremely, extremely humbled. There are literally no words that can describe mine and our thankfulness.

Chelsey

Two months ago, the Lord told me I was going to lose someone close to me. I just didn't realize it would be my sister Kyra. I didn't want to believe Him, but He constantly told me to trust Him and to lean on Him when it happens. The Lord wanted Kyra, and I don't blame Him. She is an amazing woman!

When I think about Kyra, I think about walking through her door in Italy this past Christmas and her saying, "Aunt Chelsey is here!" Where she already had my favorite lunch laid out ready to eat. Where she sat down and told me all the great and fun things that she had planned for us. Where she told me that we had a lot to do. Little did she know, I had a surprise trip planned for her and me to go to France. I planned this trip, just so I could have one-on-one sister bonding time. We grew so much closer as sisters and as best friends. We had heart-to-heart conversations when she would just encourage me in my walk with Jesus. We kept saying that we wished our other sister, Sydney, was with us. We three are pretty tight knit. We had a bond that was unbreakable. My sisters are my two best friends. Kyra was such an inspiration to both Sydney and me. We would joke around about how Sydney and I were her slaves, because if she wanted us to go to the grocery store with her at 11:00 at night, we would do it. Whatever she wanted, there we were. It's because she radiated joy at all times, and we wanted to be around her.

I remember her reading her Bible to the girls so they

could hear about Jesus. No matter how long the day was or how many dishes she had to do, she always made time to tell her girls about Jesus. Every time I visited her in Italy, I came home inspired and motivated. I noticed so much! I noticed she never raised her voice at her girls (even when I wanted to). She never complained about having to wash a million dishes at night by hand, never complained about having to walk to the grocery store with a cart *and* three small kids. That is not an easy task, let me tell you. She never complained about having to hang-dry their clothes then fold them and put them away.

Kyra cooked breakfast, lunch, dinner, dessert, and always made sure we all had a snack during the day. Between all this, she would still make time to do a hundred more things for other people. While I'm lying on the couch exhausted from just the thought that we had to do *all* this again the next day, I see Kyra continuing to go at it. She had a servant's heart and was always there for others. I came home noticing that I started staying up the extra few minutes to pick everything up and make sure my apartment was ready for the next day, just like Kyra would do.

If you didn't see my post the other day, this is what it says: "I lost my best friend, my sister, my rock. As I think about Kyra, I think about love, because her love shined in so many ways—being a loving wife, a super mom, a crazy sister, an amazing daughter, an outstanding cook, a dear friend, a child of God, and just the most incredible human being possible. She is the epitome of a godly woman, and I know my sister Sydney and I will aim to be even half the woman she was. Her life was a testimony to others."

God is so good. I lost my sister, but God is good. I have a long journey ahead of me, but God is good. I have so many questions and emotions going through my head, but God is good. I will put my firm faith and trust in the Lord today and every day after. I'm not saying it's going to be easy, because it won't be, but I will try. Sydney, I promise to do the best I can to be the big sister to you like Kyra was to both of us. Kyra exemplified Jesus in every aspect of her life. Knowing that He looked at her face to face and said, "Well done, good and faithful servant," brings joy to my heart.

The Bible describes love in 1 Corinthians 13. Where you see love, you see Kyra.

Katie

I met Kyra during my freshman year of college at UGA. Our lives grew together through every major milestone we hit. We lived together, dated our husbands together, found a church together, and traveled together. Because Kyra called a lot of places home after college, I feel unbelievably blessed that I was given many precious days alone with her before she went to her true home, because she was my best friend.

Speaking of friends, Kyra never got a Facebook account (unless she just didn't want to friend me because she knew I'd post too many personal questions). Kyra also never shopped at expensive stores. She told me she had one dress that she could wear on Sundays to their Italian church, and when she missed a recent family trip to Old Navy to come help me with my boys, she lamented over the fact that she was mad about it. She said, "I should be happy that my mom is shopping for my girls, not upset for myself. Why do I need any more clothes?"

She never was from this world. Kyra always belonged in heaven. She just didn't seem to care or get distracted by the stuff of this life. I have never known anyone like Kyra. Yet I know she wasn't perfect either. She and Reid had become food and coffee snobs since moving to Italy. Kyra told me that her sister Sydney prepared a great meal for her and

Reid recently, but she couldn't help but be disgusted by the cheese she served with it. She said it was some sort of white cheese that was pre-shredded and came in a reusable Ziploc bag! I told her that I wanted her to pick up dinner that night because everything in my fridge would disgust her.

I know I'm not the only one that learned something from Kyra, but I'm probably one of the few people that has had to be reminded that Kyra is not God. I think my own husband, while he adores Kyra, would get sick of hearing, "Well Kyra tried it, and she said it was great, so we should try it." Kyra somehow had the ability to convince me that ridiculous ideas were actually really smart. She convinced me to take a natural birthing class and forgo an epidural with my first pregnancy. She convinced me that using cloth diapers on my children was a great idea. She even convinced Reid to join a co-op and buy a cow for their raw milk supply, and I was almost ready to buy a cow myself, but then she moved to Italy, and my husband convinced me otherwise.

Kyra also imparted a lot of wisdom. She knew early on that she was called to be a wife and a mother. We talked just last week about how God had been growing her heart these last couple of years to embrace her calling even more to the point that she found pure joy in the mundane, daily rituals that most of us see as routine.

She knew that creating a home of peace and love and truth would enable her husband, whom she loved more than anyone, to spread the message of Christ with true joy and peace. She strived to show her daughters the joy of living out Christ's love every day so that they would acknowledge, love, and give their lives to Him one day.

If Kyra were here right now, she'd be telling me not to worship or idolize her, because she was a sinner just like the rest of us, and the only worshiping that should be taking place is to the One who made her.

Kyra loved her Savior like no one I've known. Her hunger to grow as a daughter of Christ affected everyone she met, and it enabled her to move closer and closer toward heaven.

While we selfishly ache to have our Kyra here longer, while some painful and confusing questions remain unanswered, and while waves of heartache feel debilitating at times, I am privileged to have been a part of Kyra's life, and I trust without a doubt that God is working mightily through her death. Not only did she change my life, but I can also stand here today saying that because of Kyra, my own mother finally accepted Christ after hearing what happened to her. The day before she died, Kyra said she would be praying for my mom and my whole family. She showed me a video called "Falling Plates" that I later showed my mom. With bittersweet joy, I am rejoicing with Kyra in heaven over another sister in Christ, whom she pointed to the cross.

Joe, Karen, Chelsey, Sydney, Reid, Nolyn, Ellie, and Livia, we love you more than you know, and Kyra loves you more than you know. When only the Holy Spirit can minister to you through groans that words cannot express, remember Lamentations 3, which continues to give me hope in all my trials:

> He has made me chew on gravel.
> He has rolled me in the dust.
> Peace has been stripped away,
> and I have forgotten what prosperity is.
> I cry out, "My splendor is gone!
> Everything I had hoped for from the Lord is lost!"
> The thought of my suffering and homelessness
> is bitter beyond words.
> I will never forget this awful time,
> as I grieve over my loss.

Yet I still dare to hope
when I remember this:
The faithful love of the Lord never ends
His mercies never cease.
Great is his faithfulness.
his mercies begin afresh each morning.
I say to myself, "The Lord is my inheritance
therefore, I will hope in him!"
The Lord is good to those who depend on him,
to those who search for him.
So it is good to wait quietly for salvation from the
Lord.

Laura

Kyra and I have been best friends for over twenty years. We grew up here at Tabernacle together. There are not many memories in my life that do not include her. We got in trouble together, like the beautiful purple stripe bathroom—sorry, Mama Karen! We went on trips together, we played together, and we were even accountability partners as we walked through our lives as wives and mothers.

I was able to have the privilege of seeing her minister in Italy a couple of years ago. Oh, what a blessing it was. What a privilege it has been to see the consistency of the Lord through her life. I have learned many things from Kyra. One of the greatest things I have learned from her is how to demonstrate God's love for others at every turn. Kyra demonstrated grace, compassion, and selflessness consistently. She was one of the most thoughtful persons I have ever known. Her hospitality was endless.

As we talked about our marriages, I learned how to pray for my husband as she prayed for hers. I watched her love, follow, and submit to Reid, as we are called to do. I watched her with her girls and saw what it really looks like to train up a child in the ways of the Lord.

I went on a walk with her and the girls last week on a very, very hot morning. The girls were miserable. Kyra kept saying how terrible an idea this was and how crazy we were for even thinking we should do this. She kept apologizing, but later I told her how encouraging it was to me to watch her respond to each incident. I knew she was frustrated, but her words and her actions never let on. At one point, she walked back to one of the girls when she just couldn't keep going, knelt down beside her, and asked if she wanted Mommy to pray with her. I stood there and watched her pray for her daughter's legs to be strengthened to finish the walk and thought, I want to be like Kyra. What grace and patience, what a shining example of how Christ cares for us.

I can't help but think of how Kyra effortlessly lived out the life of a Proverbs 31 woman:

> An excellent wife who can find? She is far more precious than jewels. The heart of her husband trusts in her, and he will have no lack of gain. She does him good, and not harm, all the days of her life. She seeks wool and flax, and works with willing hands. She is like the ships of the merchant; she brings her food from afar. She rises while it is yet night and provides food for her household and portions for maidens. She considers a field and buys it; with the fruit of her hands she plants a vineyard. She dresses herself with strength and makes her arms strong. She perceives that her merchandise is profitable. Her lamp does not go out at night. She puts her hands to the distaff, and her hands hold the spindle. She opens her hand to the poor and reaches out her hands to the needy. She is not afraid of snow for her household, for all her household is clothed in scarlet. She makes bed cov-

erings for herself; her clothing is fine linen and purple. Her husband is known in the gates when he sits among the elders of the land. She makes linen garments and sells them; she delivers sashes to the merchant. Strength and dignity are her clothing, and she laughs at the time to come. She opens her mouth with wisdom, and the teaching of kindness is on her tongue. She looks well to the way of her household and does not eat the bread of idleness. Her children rise up and call her blessed; her husband also. and he praises her. "Many women have done excellently, but you surpass them all." Charm is deceitful, and beauty is vain, but a woman who fears the Lord is to be praised. Give her the fruit of hands and let her works praise her in the gates.

May we all look to emulate Kyra's example of a life pursuing Christ and, above all, making His name known.

Leonardo De Chirico

I bring you greetings from the city of Rome, Italy, and from the Church Breccia di Roma. In Rome and in Italy there are lots of people, Christian and non-Christian, who are mourning the loss of Kyra and are standing together with Reid, Nolyn, Ellie, and Livia in this time of pain and sorrow. I have three words that capture what I think God wants me to say on this occasion. They all begin with the letter *F*: Fragrance, Fight, Forward.

Fragrance. We have been having the privilege of knowing Kyra for six years. Kyra invested the gentle, meek, and gracious person she was, and the gifts God had given her, among us. There is no better Bible verse to describe what is in our hearts: "Thanks be to God, who in Christ always leads us in triumphal procession, and through us spreads the fragrance of the knowledge of him everywhere" (2

Corinthians 2:14–15). Kyra was the fragrance of Christ in Rome. We sensed it. We breathed it. We were blessed by it. We don't know why God allowed this death to occur. One thing we know . . . she was God's gift to us, showing us the fragrance of Jesus in and through Kyra. She was so near to Christ that His aroma transpired through her. Our church and Rome will be far worse places without her.

In these six years, we have watched her and deeply admired her. She was Reid's fit helper, a caring mother, fully part of the life of the church. She was always ready to help and be at the forefront of things, though remaining humble and kind. She encouraged us to open our eyes to the tragedy of so many women who are trafficked and exploited in our streets. Her presence brought peace and grace to all she would meet.

Fight. The Bible says that all those who follow the Lord are involved in a spiritual warfare (Ephesians 6:12). Not against human beings but against the Enemy of God and his evil powers. This is true for all believers. Where is the place of the fight? Wherever God calls you to be and to serve Him. It may be in your workplace downtown, in your college; it may be overseas. Where God calls us to serve Him, *there* the devil wants to destroy and demolish the work of God. Kyra was called to serve God in Rome. She made Rome her home. Rome is a wonderful historic city, but it is also a place that is captive to powerful religious strongholds that do not want people to hear the gospel. Kyra was there to fight the good fight of the gospel with the gentleness and meekness of Christ. She would not appear as a soldier, but she was a true soldier of the gospel. Together with Reid, their colleagues, and the church, she was fighting for the truth of the gospel so that people might believe in Jesus as Lord and Savior.

Every Christian is involved in this fight, but I have seven reasons why Reid and Kyra were engaging the spiritual powers of the city of Rome in a unique and challenging way. I don't have time to go through them now, but trust me, God was using them to do something significant for the cause of the gospel. The reality of what they were doing, and its potential developments, were extraordinary for the advancement of the gospel in Rome long term.

I don't know why God allowed Kyra's death to happen. But this I know. It took place in the context of a big and violent warfare. I don't know why Kyra was taken and Reid was spared. But this I know. Though attacked, God was in control and His victory secured. Dying on the cross for our sins and raising from the death for our justification, Jesus Christ won the victory over Satan and sin. As Martin Luther wrote in his famous hymn, "A Mighty Fortress Is Our God":

> Let goods and kindred go, this mortal life also;
> The body they may kill: God's plan abideth still,
> His kingdom is forever.

The kingdom shall be God's and will belong to His people.

Forward. Fragrance, Fight, Forward. We stand in awe and tears for what happened to Kyra and the Karr family. The standing question remains: what is going to happen now? I am sure that if Kyra would be here, she would say, "Go forward! Continue to trust God! Continue to believe in Him and serve Him!" It is not only Kyra, but God wants us to move forward. God's history always moves forward. There is hope for Kyra. Even now, she stands in God's blessed presence. She was prepared to come home to Rome, but God took her to the heavenly home. In her smile she anticipated the wonders of God, and now she sees Him face to face. Kyra's smile was a window open for us on the heavenly realities. Her last cry was immediately transformed into a song of praise to God.

There will be a time in which Kyra's body will be raised again and together with all the saints of Rome, Cartersville, and wherever else; she will sing the praises of her Savior, the Lord of Lords and the King of Kings. Forward is also the word that she would say to her family. Reid, forward with God. Nolyn, Ellie, Livia, forward to become women of faith, grace, and courage, like your mummy.

Because the love of God compels us and being encouraged by her example, we in Rome will continue the work that God had called Kyra to do. There will be a time in which a strong community of believers in Jesus Christ will worship the triune God in San Paolo and elsewhere in Rome. We commit ourselves to carrying on the task that God had given to Kyra. Death does not have the final word. God always does! His plan will prevail. His will shall be done.

Thank you, God, for Kyra, for her desire to live among us spreading around us the fragrance of Christ to fight the good fight of the gospel, and for pointing upward to you and forward to your Kingdom.

Pastor Don Hattaway

You have heard many testimonies this morning about how Kyra was a very special person, and she was. It's been mentioned that she was a precious daughter, an incredible sister, an excellent mother, a loving wife, a great friend, and a passionate missionary. I can add one other thing to that list: she was a lifesaver. Perhaps you don't know that she actually saved my life when I was in Rome. We traveled there back in June. A number of us had a great time. They eat pasta in Rome. It is very good, but we had been eating it for about a week, for breakfast, dinner, and supper. On one particular day, it had been very hot. We were out in the streets ministering to people, and it had been a long day. We finally made our way back to Reid and Kyra's apartment. We had to walk up four or five flights of stairs, and we were so hungry and weakened that we started asking the blessing as we were going up the stairs. Being from Georgia, I was ready for some beef, and I was expecting Kyra to say we were going to have pasta. Instead, she said we were going to have sloppy joes. I want you to know that we ate like kings that night, and it literally saved my life! What a great hostess she was, and just a precious, precious soul.

But what is it that made Kyra so special? What was it? It all started back when she was nine years old. She came to the place in her life where she realized that she was a sinner. And that's hard to believe for us. Kyra seemed perfect, but she was not perfect. She was like all of us: she needed a Savior. The Bible says we have all sinned and come short of the glory of God. Even the best among us is in need of a Savior. She realized that she needed Christ. She read in the Bible that Jesus is the only way to be saved. He is the way, the truth, and the life, and no man comes to the Father but through Christ. With childlike faith, she acknowledged before the Lord that she was a sinner, and she trusted Jesus to forgive her of her sins. She surrendered her life to Christ. From that moment on, she started a process of growth and development that took her to this point where we are today. Her life was changed. If she were standing here today, I am convinced that she would say to you, "Come to Christ. Trust Jesus as your Savior. You can't make it without Him. You can't be saved without Christ." That would be her appeal to you today. She gave her life to that message. She was indeed special.

Because Kyra was a follower of Christ, everything in her life was influenced by her relationship with Jesus Christ.

In thinking about her life, my mind goes to a woman in the Bible named Mary of Bethany. There are several Marys in the Bible. This is Mary who is the sister of Lazarus and Martha. She is mentioned only three times in the Bible, but each time she is found sitting at the feet of Jesus.

Notice, first of all, Mary's fellowship at Jesus's feet. In Luke 10:38–42, we find the story of Jesus fellowshipping in the home of Lazarus, Martha, and Mary. Martha was a servant. She loved to cook. She was in the kitchen a lot. She was getting frustrated because Mary was sitting at the feet of Jesus absorbing everything He had to say, just enjoying her fellowship with her Lord. So she came out of the kitchen, wiped her hands on her apron, and asked Jesus to tell Mary to get up and come help her in the kitchen. Notice Jesus's response in verses 41–42: but the Lord answered and said to her, 'Martha, Martha, you are worried and bothered about so many things; but only one thing is necessary; for Mary has chosen the good part, which shall not be taken away from her." Jesus was not criticizing Martha for serving—that's a worthy thing to do—but He was pointing out that true service comes from an overflowing heart. Mary was filling up her heart in the presence of Christ so that when she did serve, she would be able to serve as an overflow of what Christ was doing in her as a follower . . . as a true disciple of Jesus. That's how Kyra lived. She spent time with Jesus, fellowshipping with Him, enjoying His presence, absorbing what He had to say as she devoted herself to the study of God's Word and prayer.

I think also about Mary's hardship at Jesus's feet. In John chapter 11 we find a very sad story, at least initially. It's the story of Lazarus's death. Martha and Mary were concerned that their brother was going to die if Jesus did not return. They sent word for Him to come back and intervene because without Jesus their brother would die. Jesus intentionally delayed His return and Lazarus did die. As a matter of fact, when Jesus returned, Lazarus had been dead for four days and his body had already begun to stink. Martha comes out and greets Jesus and then she is followed by Mary. Notice what Mary does when she sees Jesus: "Therefore when Mary came where Jesus was, she saw Him and fell at His feet saying to Him, 'Lord, if you'd have been here, my brother wouldn't have died.'"

Maybe there are some of you who are here this morning and asking, "Where was Jesus on Thursday night? If Jesus is so powerful, if God is so strong, why didn't He intervene? Why didn't He do something?" As was the case in this passage, it is true for us today. God had greater plans in mind. Notice as we continue to read in this passage: "When Jesus, therefore, saw her weeping, and the Jews who came with her also weeping, He was deeply moved in spirit and was troubled." Do you feel troubled today? Are you moved in your spirit? I don't know about you, but while sitting here listening to these young ladies share their hearts about their relationship with Kyra, and this dear pastor about how Kyra and Reid have been used by God in such a powerful way in Rome, my heart was stirred. I was troubled inside, and my emotions are raw, just as yours are.

But notice what Jesus did. The Bible states, "Jesus said, 'Where have you laid him? And they said to Him, Lord, come and see.'" And then the Bible tells us, the shortest verse in the Bible, "Jesus wept." Jesus did not weep because He felt hopeless. He knew what He was going to do. He knew He was going to raise Lazarus. He had the power to do it. He wept because He felt the sense of loss that His dear friends were feeling. He saw their anguish. He saw their suffering, and He could identify with them. He wept with them. And I want you to know that Jesus is weeping with you today. He knows how you feel. He knows the loss that you've encountered, and He cares. He's concerned. Of course, the story continues as Jesus went to that tomb. He prayed to the Father and said, "Lazarus come forth," and appearing in the mouth of that tomb was Lazarus, freshly raised from the dead. Jesus did that because He's the resurrection and the life, and Jesus Himself said, "If any man believes in me, even though he dies yet shall he live." I am happy to tell you today that Jesus Christ is still the resurrection and the life. Because of His power and the fact that He has conquered death, hell, and the grave, we have the certain expectation that we will see Kyra again. There is no question in my mind.

I also think of Mary's worship at Jesus's feet. In John 12:1–8, again we find Jesus with His friends Lazarus, Martha, and Mary. They were having a meal together. They did not sit at a table the way we do today. They lounged around a low table, propped up on an elbow, stretched out, eating with the other hand. I kind of like that approach. I think maybe we should go back to that. Well, that is the scene. They were lying around the table eating and without a lot of commotion, without any notice, Mary entered the room. The Bible tells us in verse 3, "Mary took a pound of very costly perfume of pure nard and anointed the feet of Jesus and wiped His feet with her hair; and the house was filled with the fragrance of the perfume."

She took the most valuable thing she had and poured it out on the feet of Jesus. Then she took her hair and wiped His feet. Mary did that because she had learned something while sitting at the feet of Jesus. He was going to the cross. She was anointing His feet before His burial. The disciples missed it. We know this because they had been arguing about who would be first in the kingdom. Jesus took a basin of water and a towel and begins to wash His disciples' feet. Although the disciples missed the opportunity to wash His feet prior to the crucifixion, Mary did not. She did it as an expression of worship. She poured out her best perfume, and everyone in the room was impacted. The fragrance of that perfume permeated that entire setting. Isn't that just like Kyra? Pouring out herself in the lives of others, and the aroma, the fragrance of her service, and her worship of her Lord have influenced all of us. That is why she was so special. It is because she spent time at the feet of Jesus, and her life was changed. She was a follower of Christ, a disciple of the Lord.

I think I can capture the essence of Kyra's life with one photograph taken when we were in Rome in June. She is kneeling before some children, in a position of humility. She has a Bible in her hand. She is reading from that Bible because she believes it is the Word of God, and it is. She is sharing what she has learned at the feet of Jesus. In the picture, she takes her other hand and uses it to drive the point home of her teaching. There is passion in her words and even in her expressions. She is telling those children about Christ. You say, "Well, where is Kyra today? Where is she?" Psalm 116:15 tells us, "Precious in the sight of the Lord is the death of His saints." God views death differently from us. We see death as the end, but it is not the end. Jesus has conquered death.

Death is the doorway through which we pass into His presence. For the believer, it is not the time to grieve as those who have no hope. Yes, we weep because our hearts are heavy, but we rejoice because we know Christ is the victor. Where is she now? Paul said in 2 Corinthians 5:8 concerning Christians, "to be absent from the body is to be in God's presence." The body is left, but she is not here; she has gone to be with Christ. She is in His presence. Where is she now? I'll tell you where she is. She is where she has been since she was nine years old. She's sitting at the feet of Jesus.

Father, we thank you for your presence in this place today. We thank you for the testimony of a life well-lived. We thank you for Kyra. She has touched all of us, Lord. If she were standing here today, she would appeal for people to come to know Jesus as Savior and Lord the way she knows Him. Hearing all these testimonies and compliments, she would be pointing to you and saying it is all because of Jesus. Lord, we rejoice in her life. We celebrate her life. Lord, we look forward to what you are going to do here at Tabernacle, through our convention and through the body of Christ here and in Rome. You are going to use this to fan the flame of missions for reaching the world for Christ. And Father, we pray that you comfort this family today. Strengthen them for the work that lies ahead. We believe it will not be long until we will all be in your presence worshipping and praising you together. We look forward to that day. We praise you for this day. In Jesus's name, we pray. Amen.

Joe

As Reid has conveyed, from our family and the Karr family, we thank our dear friends, we thank our church family, who has been incredible the last four or five days, and we thank this community. Without the outpouring of love and support that we've seen, I don't know how we could have made it through these last five days. So we thank you and we love you.

I was thinking about what to share, and the Lord took me off the hook. He said, well, just share what Kyra would want you to share. So that got me off the hook for saying what I wanted to say. Basically, it comes down to really two thoughts—two very simple thoughts that she would want me to say here today, as we close and leave here.

You know, it seems today in the world's environment, religion seems to be the focus of everyone's attention, and it's usually because of current events that happen. Recently the Supreme Court decision on homosexuality has raised the discussion of religion. You can go back to the mid-sixties, and the decision of the court case, Roe vs. Wade, on abortion, heightened the discussion of religion. And we have Christianity, we have the fast growth of the faith of Islam, we have Buddhism, Hinduism, atheism, agnostics, and every religion in between. If you were to Google "religions of the world," there would probably come up hundreds and hundreds, maybe even thousands of religions of the world.

Today, the logical question would be this: Who's right, and who's wrong? But as I stand here, that's not the question at all. The question is, what's the truth?

You know, when we look at the Bible and at Christianity, people look at the Old Testament and they kind of scoff and laugh. "These are just old fairy tales, you know. They may be applicable thousands of years ago. There's really nothing to them." And in the New Testament, they say, "Well, there's a lot of talk about love in the New Testament." And love seems to be applied to justify a lot of things in the world today. It's all about love.

Men have discussed these religions over the centuries. Men have debated these for centuries. Men have fought over all these religions for centuries. And ultimately, men have died over all these religions.

I gave my life to Christ when I was twenty-five years old. He didn't change my quirky, stupid personality. Just ask my daughters and anyone who knows me. Still stupid, still tell stupid jokes. Everyone thinks I'm not funny. My daughters laugh, just a kind of token laugh just to make me happy.

He didn't do that; He transformed my life. I'm still the same sinful man, but one day when I stand before Him, because I accepted Christ and what He did for us and all of us, I will be in heaven with Kyra one day.

Kyra would just want me to ask one question for everybody who hasn't done that. Who is this Jesus that the Bible talks about? Who is He? It's either true or it's not true when it comes right down to it. You either believe or you don't. And if you don't look at it, or you ignore it, you've already answered the question. So Kyra would just want me to ask that one question to everybody here today who hasn't done that. Examine the evidence.

And finally, as I stand here in this situation today, I, along with my wonderful, beautiful wife; my two precious daughters, Sydney and Chelsey; Reid; Reid's mother, Janet; and Reid's brother and sisters, stand here today, and without a shadow of a doubt know that God orchestrated this whole event. If the world was listening, they would say, "You're crazy!" But he did orchestrate it, 100 percent. He's done it for His glory. We don't understand it. That's the Rock we are standing on.

We're standing on the Rock, and we can't wait to see what God is going to do with this. We are going to give Him all the glory and all the praise. As Pastor Leo said, we're going to move forward.

21

Ripples on the Water

I always enjoyed watching my sons skip rocks in water when they were young. The bigger the body of water, the better the rock's potential to make more ripples. My granddaughter and I now enjoy the same activity. It is a fun and simple thing we can enjoy together. Part of the fun is collecting the rocks to skip. The rocks have to be just the right size and weight. The goal of rock skipping is to get as many ripples as possible. My granddaughter and I always jump with joy when we see more than three ripples from our rock. We jump high and squeal loudly when our rock makes six or more ripples.

Kyra didn't collect rocks, but she did depend on the Rock of her life. She didn't have to hunt for a collection of things to bring her joy. She had the One who filled her soul every day with His love. She obeyed His beckoning. It was as if she were skipping a pebble of love from her main

Rock to those around her. She looked for little places as well as big places for opportunities to give His love away, and each giveaway had a ripple effect. Kyra's thirty years of life produced more ripples of love than the life of some whose lifespan tripled hers.

Kyra has now heard the words of Jesus, "Well done, good and faithful servant" (Matthew 25:21). Kyra's place of residence may have changed, but the ripples of her life continue.

When Reid and Kyra were called to Rome, she was dedicated 100 percent. She knew it would be hard but was no less committed, knowing what it would take to plant or build churches in Rome. This commitment was rooted in her love for God and His gospel and in her love for the Italian people.

Would the death of Kyra stop the work that she and Reid had begun in Rome? Or would her early homegoing be a catalyst of ripples to make spiritual waves in Rome?

Reid Returns to Rome without Kyra

A few weeks after Kyra's death, Reid returned to Rome with his three little girls in tow. His friends and coworkers watched his life. They knew that Reid, as a mere human, could not return to Rome without Kyra unless something or Someone was helping him. They observed that just because Kyra was gone from this earthly home, it did not mean that Reid's call to Rome had disappeared.

Kyra's Ripples

Below are a few of the ripples of Kyra's life. The ripples continue today, and through her family and friends, they will forever be flowing.

Katie's Mom

From the beginning of her friendship with Katie during college, Kyra had encouraged her friend to grow in her faith. Katie's family had not known their desperate need for a Savior, so surrendering their lives to an unseen God was a foreign concept they could not embrace. Unknown to Katie, Kyra prayed for her family's salvation.

A decade later, Kyra continued to encourage Katie. She shared a powerful video that she had seen in Italy. Not long after Kyra's death, Katie showed the same video, "Falling Plates," to her mother, Debbie. Because of its gospel message and the faithful prayers of two dear friends across the years, Debbie put her faith in Jesus Christ.

Kyra was intentional in sharing the gospel of Jesus Christ, in word and deed, to those in her sphere of influence. She recognized that she was not responsible for the outcome, but her obedience created the unforeseen yet hoped for ripple.

Helena, Luca, and Pablo

For Helena and her husband, Luca, watching Reid deal with his pain and suffering was as powerful a testimony as watching Kyra live out her faith. Helena testifies, "The way Reid adapted to life without Kyra and how he learned to take care of the girls without the support of their thoughtful mommy was witness to the power of the Holy Spirit working in and through him."

Today Helena, Luca, and their son, Pablo, are faithfully serving at the Brecca church plant in San Paulo. What a beautiful ripple from a painful storm.

The Kyra Karr Foundation

Reid and Kyra's families knew that the ripples of Kyra's life could not be measured. They wisely set up a foundation in her honor, with all the donations to the foundation going to the ongoing work in Rome. Kyra's commitment to Rome lives on through offerings given to the foundation.

Kyra's youngest sister, Sydney, oversees the daily operation of the foundation's website and communication. Sydney witnesses the ripples of Kyra's life every time she opens her computer to work.

Breccia di Roma's New Building

We really do not have any idea if Kyra sees what is happening here on earth. But if she does, this is one ripple that I believe gives her great joy. She had longed for her church, Breccia di Roma, to have their own building. The Kyra Karr Foundation made her dream a reality. After over one hundred years, the first evangelical church of its kind opened in Rome. Breccia di Roma was able to buy their own building just around the corner from where they rented the basement of the Waldensian church.

The storefront building needed a makeover with some reconstruction. When the renovation was complete in 2017, the building was dedicated to Kyra's memory.

Steppie Steps into the Picture

This ripple of love is one that might cause Kyra to rejoice with her unique kind of enthusiasm. God sent Reid a loving wife and a mother to love and care for Nolyn, Ellie, and Livia. Stephanie Lorin Williams, lovingly called Steppie, was born the same year as Kyra. She grew up in Memphis, Tennessee, and her family attended Bellevue Baptist Church at the same time as Kyra and her family. As a blonde-haired first grader, she received her first Bible, signed by Adrian Rogers, the same day that Kyra got hers.

Steppie had never married, though she had turned down a proposal when she didn't feel God's peace to say yes. Steppie felt fulfilled in her life, but inwardly she wished that God would bless her with a family of her own. Before she met Reid, she and her brother were discussing her single-ness. During that conversation, her brother said, "Maybe God has a widower with children waiting somewhere in the world to meet you." Indeed, He did.

A mutual friend introduced Steppie and Reid while she was serving in Greece with the same company as Reid. Their first months of getting to know each other consisted of communication over the internet. Their wedding took place in November of 2018. She immediately stepped into role of wife, mom, and missionary to Rome.

In 2020, due to the COVID-19 pandemic, Steppie went alone to a Rome hospital to deliver their first son, Philip Reid Karr V, lovingly called Kip.

Ellie's Testimony

Nolyn, Ellie, and Livia lived their early childhoods secure in ripples of the deep love of their mother, nurtured by her faith in Jesus Christ. In time, they were embraced by the love of a new mom. On the day of her baptism, ten-year-old Ellie gave this testimony:

> I have come here today to share with you all that I believe in God and that Jesus died on the cross for my sins. But there's something else. God has also made me very happy, because when my mom Kyra died, God gave me a new mom, Steppie. And so for all these things I have come here today to be baptized. Thank you.

Karen, Joe, Chelsey, and Sydney embrace Steppie as their own. The ripples of love that formed Kyra continue to be passed to Nolyn, Ellie, and Livia.

22

Conclusione

(Conclusion in Italian)

Six years ago, when I began this writing journey, I had three goals. First, I wanted to encourage my friends Karen and Joe. Second, I wanted to dedicate something about Kyra to Nolyn, Ellie, and Livia. The last goal was to figure out how Kyra and Reid's families faced such a huge tragedy with indescribable strength and grace.

My three goals have been met, but there was one thing that I did not expect—my view on life and death have changed. Through the many interviews and the reading of Kyra's journal, I have learned so much from her thirty years on earth. I am changed from one who complicated the day-to-day challenges of life to one who surrenders the unanswerable questions. I now also see the value of not trying to change those I love. My only responsibility is to authentically love them. Finally, I found the joy that can come from surrendered brokenness.

My friend, Nathan Hattaway, emailed the following verse to Karen soon after Kyra's death:

"The righteous perish, and no one takes it to heart; the devout are taken away, and no one understands that the righteous are taken away to be spared from evil" (Isaiah 57:1).

Did God spare Kyra from something evil? None of us know for sure, but we do know that even when things are unclear, we can choose which filter to sift our grief through—bitterness or betterment. The Carps and Karrs chose betterment.

Thank you to all I interviewed to make this book possible, and thank you to Karen and Joe for entrusting me with telling your daughter's story.

Thank you, Kyra, for all the things you taught me from your simple, yet strong, surrender to Jesus. Matthew 25 talks about the kingdom of heaven. In memory of Kyra, I quote verse 21, "Well done, good and faithful servant."

Recipes from Kyra

Kyra was always giving happies—or little gifts—to those around her.

The following recipes are a gift from Kyra's kitchen to you. Enjoy.

Apple Vinaigrette Salad Dressing

When I visited Kyra in Rome, she served our team a delicious fresh salad with the best dressing I had ever tasted. Kyra made the dressing from scratch. She wrote down the recipe for me. I later learned that she had also shared this recipe with friends Melody Pendley and Sonny Hattaway. Now we would like to share it with you.

Ingredients:
One peeled apple
½ cup olive oil
¼ cup apple cider vinegar
¼ cup honey

½ tsp minced garlic (garlic powder works)
Salt and pepper to taste

Blend all ingredients except the salt and pepper in a small bowl to your preferred consistency. Pour over salad. Add salt and pepper.

This dressing is great over any salad greens. Add toasted almonds, diced apples, green onions, or anything else you want.

Sharon's Sausage Stars

One of Kyra's favorite recipes was given to her by her Sunday school teacher, Sharon Mauldin. Sharon brought sausage stars for every *Breakfast Sunday*, which was the first Sunday of the month. Kyra and the rest of the ninth graders devoured the scrumptious appetizers.

Ingredients:
2 cups (1 lb.) cooked sausage, crumbled
1 ½ cups shredded cheddar cheese
1 ½ cups shredded Monterey Jack
1 cup ranch dressing
½ cup chopped bell pepper
1 package wonton wrappers
Cooking spray or brushed oil

Preheat oven to 350 degrees. Mix cooked sausage with cheese, ranch dressing, and peppers. Lightly grease muffin tin. Press one wonton into each cup. (The wontons come out looking like stars.) Lightly brush or spray with oil. Bake for 5 minutes or until golden. Remove from muffin tin and place on a baking sheet. Fill each wonton with sausage mixture and bake 5 more minutes or until bubbly. Each recipe yields 3–4 dozen depending on how many wontons are in package.

Amatriciana

This dish was submitted by Kyra's sister Chelsey Carp, and Kyra's friend and IMB Journeymen missionary Elizabeth Cassada. Kyra's family requested Amatriciana quite often.

Ingredients:
500 grams (1 lb.) mezze maniche pasta or rigatoni
Olive oil (about 2 T or enough to coat bottom of pan)
1 tsp. crushed red pepper, pepperoncino, or red pepper flakes
1 onion, chopped
250 grams (3 packages) pancetta or 1 ½ cups bacon
½ cup white wine (Kyra's terminology was "a glug")
2 cans crushed tomatoes or half sauce and half chopped tomatoes
1 tsp. salt and pepper
¼ cup grated Pecorino, Romano, or Parmesan cheese

Bring water to boil in a large pot. Add salt and pasta and cook according to package instructions. Heat olive oil in separate saucepan until hot. Add a nickel-sized amount of crushed red pepper and cook in oil for 30 seconds. Add onion and bacon or pancetta. Sauté until golden brown, stirring occasionally. Crank the heat up, add wine, and scrape off bottom of pan. Turn heat back down to low and add crushed tomatoes and cheese. Let simmer half an hour, stirring occasionally. If you're using chopped tomatoes, add them here. Serve sauce over pasta with grated cheese.

Orechiette with Sausage, Beans, and Mascarpone

This dish was often requested by Kyra's family and friends in Italy.

Ingredients:
500 grams (1 lb.) orecchiette pasta
2 T olive oil
250 grams (½ lb.) sausage
1 small onion
425 grams cannellini beans, drained and rinsed
2 T oregano, chopped
½ cup mascarpone
1 tsp. salt
½ tsp. ground pepper

Cook pasta in salted boiling water. Sauté onion and sausage in olive oil until golden brown and sausage is in tiny pieces. Add beans and oregano. Cook for 2 minutes. Add a cup of pasta water and stir, scraping bits from the bottom of the pan. Add mascarpone and stir well until melted. Add salt, pepper, and hot pasta.

Risotto di Zucca (Pumpkin Risotto)

This dish reflects Kyra's love for cooking with fresh ingredients. When we were at the Italian grocery store, she showed me the difference between Italian pasta and American pasta. The Italian pasta ingredients were cleaner. Kyra's friend Katie called her the food Nazi, as she always encouraged fresh foods. This Italian dish was also a favorite with family and friends.

The recipe originated from the kitchen of the Hotel Cipriani in Venice, Chef Renato Piccolotto.

Ingredients:
600 grams (1 lb. 5 oz.) fresh pumpkin, chopped into very small chunks
2 T olive oil
90 grams (3 ¼ oz.) butter
2 chopped and 2 full sprigs fresh rosemary
1 garlic glove
1 small onion, finely chopped
30 grams (10 ½ oz.) Carnaroli rice
1 liter (1 ¾ pints) chicken stock, hot
50 grams (2 oz.) Parmesan cheese, freshly grated
Salt and pepper to taste

In a pan, heat oil and a third of the butter, then add the whole sprigs of rosemary, garlic clove, and pumpkin. The pumpkin will automatically exude some liquid, and water will need to be added. Cook for about 20 minutes or until pumpkin softens and dissolves. Remove rosemary sprigs and garlic clove.

In another large pan, heat half the remaining butter and fry the onion gently until soft. Then add rice and fry equally as gently, stirring continuously for a few minutes. Add a little of the hot chicken stock, then the pumpkin mixture. Gradually add more stock until it is all used up and has been absorbed by the rice, stirring from time to time to avoid it sticking to the pan. Take off heat and beat in remaining butter and parmesan. Sprinkle with chopped rosemary. Serves 4.

Northern Bean and Ham Soup

This is a recipe that Kyra gave to her one of her best friends, Laura McCoy. Laura enjoys serving this delicious soup to her family and friends. It can be cooked on a stove top or in a crock-pot.

Ingredients:
2 tsp. olive oil
1 small yellow sweet onion, chopped
2 garlic cloves, minced
1 ½ cups diced cooked ham
4 cans great northern beans (14 oz.) or 1 ½ lbs. cooked dry beans
3 cups chicken broth
1 tsp. salt adjust to taste

Stovetop
Heat olive oil in large pot over medium heat, add onion, and cook until tender. Add garlic and ham; sauté for about one minute. Add chicken broth and half of the beans. Salt to taste. Cook over medium to low heat for at least 1 ½ hours. Blend soup from pot with a food processor or blender. Add remaining beans to soup and simmer for another 10–15 minutes. Makes 8–10 servings.

Crock-pot
Heat olive oil in skillet over medium heat, add onion, and cook until tender. Add garlic and ham and sauté for about one minute.

Transfer this mixture to large crock-pot. Add chicken broth and half of beans. Salt to taste. Cook on low for 4 hours. Blend soup with food processor or blender. Add remaining beans to soup and cook on low for 1–2 hours. Makes 8–10 servings.

Sloppy Joes

Kyra's sloppy joes became famous, at least to Pastor Don Hattaway. When Pastor Don, his son Nathan, and Kyra's Daddy Joe were visiting Reid and Kyra, their week was full of helping the missionaries anyway they could. One day they were famished and exhausted from their ministry assignment. Don and the team smelled the food cooking the minute they entered the apartment building. They could not climb the four flights of stairs fast enough. Expecting another pot of Italian pasta, they were pleasantly surprised to see the sloppy joes on the table. Out of all the delicious food on that trip, Kyra's sloppy joes stood out and will never be forgotten.

Ingredients:
1 ½ lbs. ground beef
1 diced onion
½ cup ketchup
1 tsp. dry mustard
1 T sugar
1 tsp. Worcestershire sauce
1 T vinegar

Brown meat with onion. Whisk together remaining ingredients. Drain meat. Pour sauce over meat and simmer until time to serve. Serve on hamburger buns.

Prayer Bar Candy

The next three recipes were submitted by Kyra's mom, Karen. The family gift of hospitality was clearly passed on to Kyra. The time it takes to make them reveal the love that goes into each serving. Prayer Bar Candy is from Kyra's great-grandmother (Karen's grandmother).

First Layer
1 stick butter, melted
4 T cocoa
½ cup powdered sugar
1 egg, beaten
1 tsp. vanilla extract
½ cups nuts (walnuts or pecans work best)
1 cup shredded sweetened coconut
2 cups graham crackers, crushed

Melt butter. Add cocoa, powdered sugar, beaten egg, and vanilla extract. Mix all ingredients together and press into a 9x13 pan.

Second Layer
1 stick butter, melted
6 T heavy whipping cream
2 tsp. dry vanilla instant pudding
4 cups powdered sugar

Mix melted butter, cream, and instant pudding. Cook for about 1 minute, stirring constantly. Remove from heat and add powdered sugar. Beat well and spread over first layer.

Third Layer
1 standard sized Hershey chocolate bar

Melt chocolate bar and pour over second layer. Chill well. Cut in small pieces.

Ice Cream Pie

This recipe began with Kyra's grandmother on Karen's side. Kyra often requested this pie.

Ingredients:
½ gallon of ice cream of your choice

Crust
1 box of vanilla wafers, crushed
1 cup pecans or walnuts, chopped
1 ½ stick butter, melted

In large bowl, mix all ingredients and press into 9x13 pan until firm on the bottom. Spread ice cream over crust. Cover and place in freezer.

Chocolate Sauce
1 cup sugar
2 T cocoa
1 cup heavy whipping cream

Cook until thickened. When ready to serve, spoon over each individual slice of pie.

Chocolate Peanut Butter Pie

Kyra shared this family favorite with her family and friends. She first tasted it in her mom's kitchen.

Ingredients:
8 oz. cream cheese
1 cup powdered sugar
¾ cup whole milk
1 tsp. vanilla extract
1 cup heavy whipping cream
3–4 Butterfinger candy bars, crushed
1 chocolate pie crust

Beat cream cheese, powdered sugar, and peanut butter until smooth. Slowly mix in milk and vanilla. In separate bowl, beat whipping cream until thickened. Fold cream into peanut butter mixture. Stir crushed candy bars into mixture. Spoon mixture into chocolate crust. Cover and freeze. Remove from freezer about 10 minutes before serving.

"I Surrender All"

Refrain: I surrender all, I surrender all;

All to Thee, my blessed Savior,

I surrender all.

—Judson W. Van De Venter (1896)

Thank you for reading Kyra's "Simple Surrender" story. Kyra knew how to face the pain and complications of life and faith. She made her life about one word: *surrender*. Surrender to the one who gave her abundant life.

All proceeds of this book go to KyraKarrFoundation.com.

ORDER INFORMATION

To order additional copies of this book, please visit
www.redemption-press.com.
Also available at Christian bookstores and Barnes and Noble.

Printed in the USA
CPSIA information can be obtained
at www.ICGtesting.com
LVHW101140180823
755120LV00002B/10